quick breads

quick breads

Liz Franklin

photography by Jean Cazals

Served warm from the oven, there are few things more tempting than **sweet quick breads 6**. A bowl of soup and a crisp side salad are natural partners for **savoury quick breads 36**. Capture the flavours of the festive season when you're baking **celebration quick breads 68**. Can't find that recipe? Check the **index 94**.

Sweet Quick Breads

Tangy Triple Citrus Loaf

Makes 1 x 900 g/2 lb loaf
Preparation time 2¼ hours, including cooling
and icing
You will need a loaf pan with a 900 g/2 lb/8-cup
capacity, lightly buttered and base-lined with baking
parchment or greaseproof paper

250 g/9 oz/2¼ sticks butter
250 g/9 oz/1¼ cups caster (superfine) sugar
3 eggs, beaten
300 g/10 oz/2½ cups self-raising flour
grated zest and juice 1 lemon
juice 1 lime
grated zest and juice 1 orange

topping
300 g/10 oz/2½ cups icing (confectioners') sugar
6 passion fruit
1 tablespoon butter, softened

My son, Tim, adores this loaf; it has all the fresh flavours of tangy citrus juices, finished off with a wonderful, fragrant passion fruit icing. We like the crunch the little passion-fruit seeds add to the icing, but you could sift them out if you prefer.

Preheat the oven to 180°C/350°F/Gas mark 4. In a large bowl, cream together the butter and sugar until light and fluffy. Beat in the eggs, a little at a time, until fully incorporated (simply add a little of the flour if the mixture seems to be curdling). Once the eggs have been added, stir in the remaining flour, the lemon zest and juice, the lime juice and the orange zest and juice.

Spoon the mixture evenly into the prepared pan. Bake for about 1 hour 10 minutes, but check after 1 hour. The loaf should be risen and golden and a skewer should come out clean when inserted into the centre.

Leave to cool in the pan for 30 minutes, and then turn onto a wire rack and leave until cold.

To make the topping, sift the icing (confectioners') sugar into a large bowl. Scoop out the pulp and seeds from the passion fruit and stir this into the icing (confectioners') sugar. Beat in the butter. Drizzle the icing over the cooled loaf and leave to set. Store in an airtight container.

Banana and Chocolate Chip Loaf

Makes 1 x 900 g/2 lb loaf
Preparation time 1½ hours, plus cooling
You will need a loaf pan with a 900 g/2 lb/8-cup capacity, lightly buttered and base-lined with baking parchment or greaseproof paper

120 g/4 oz/1 stick butter
150 g/5 oz/⅔ cup caster (superfine) sugar
2 bananas, mashed
2 eggs, beaten
250 g/9 oz/2¼ cups self-raising flour
1 teaspoon ground cinnamon
100 g/3½ oz/½ cup dark chocolate chips

The best bananas to use in any banana bread or cake are the ones that are so ripe they have turned black – just at the point when so many people think they are useless and throw them out. No! This is the time when the flavour is so sweet and intense that they impart such a glorious flavour. Pop them in the freezer and when you come to use them, they will thaw with a lovely squishy texture that is just perfect for stirring straight into a cake batter.

Preheat the oven to 180°C/350°F/Gas mark 4. Cream the butter and sugar together in a large bowl. Stir in the mashed bananas and beat in the eggs gradually, one at a time. Add the flour and cinnamon and stir well until smooth. Fold in the chocolate chips.

Pour the mixture into the prepared pan and bake for about 1 hour 10 minutes, or until a skewer inserted into the centre of the loaf comes out clean.

Leave to cool in the pan for about 20 minutes, and then turn onto a wire rack and leave to cool completely. Store in an airtight container. This loaf freezes beautifully.

Lemon-iced Poppy Seed Loaf

Makes 1 x 900 g/2 lb loaf
Preparation time 2½ hours, including cooling
and icing
You will need a loaf pan with a 900 g/2 lb/8-cup
capacity, lightly buttered and base-lined with baking
parchment or greaseproof paper

250 g/9 oz/2¼ sticks butter
250 g/9 oz/1¼ cups caster (superfine) sugar
4 eggs, beaten
250 g/9 oz/2¼ cups self-raising flour
grated zest and juice 1 lemon
100 g/3½ oz/⅔ cup poppy seeds

icing
250 g/9 oz/2¼ cups icing (confectioners') sugar
grated zest and juice 2 small lemons

Poppy seeds add a fabulous texture to loaves and cakes, and the lovely lemon icing complements the gentle crunch perfectly. Perfect for summer picnics or tucked into a lunch box, it also makes a great accompaniment to a good pot of afternoon tea.

Preheat the oven to 180°C/350°F/Gas mark 4. Cream the butter and sugar together until light and fluffy. Add the eggs, a little at a time, stirring in between each addition, until the mixture is smooth and all the eggs have been incorporated. Stir in the flour, and then beat in the lemon juice and zest and the poppy seeds.

Spoon the mixture into the prepared pan and bake for about 1 hour 10 minutes, or until golden and springy to the touch.

Remove from the oven and leave to cool for about 20 minutes in the pan. Turn onto a wire rack and leave until completely cold.

To make the icing, sift the icing (confectioners') sugar into a large bowl and add the lemon zest and enough of the lemon juice to give the icing the texture of thick pouring (heavy) cream. Spread the icing over the cold loaf using a palette knife (metal spatula) and leave until set. Store in an airtight container.

Intensely Orange Ginger Loaf

Makes 1x 900 g/2 lb loaf
Preparation time 1 hour 20 minutes, plus cooling
You will need a loaf pan with a 900 g/2 lb/8-cup
capacity, lightly buttered and base-lined with baking
parchment or greaseproof paper

250 g/9 oz/¾ cup golden syrup
200 ml/7 fl oz/1 cup crème fraîche
150 g/5 oz/¾ cup dark muscovado (dark brown) sugar
2 eggs, beaten
1½ tablespoons ground ginger
grated zest 2 oranges
250 g/9 oz/1 cup butter, melted and cooled
300 g/10 oz/2½ cups plain (all-purpose) flour
2 teaspoons baking powder
100 g/3½ oz crystallized ginger, roughly chopped

This is a delicious dark, sticky loaf, with chunks
of crystallized ginger dotted throughout, and
lots of tangy orange zest, which makes a lovely
combination with the hot zingy ginger. I think
this loaf is perfect served unadorned, with a nice
cup of tea and the newspaper.

Preheat the oven to 180°C/350°F/Gas mark 4. In a large
bowl, beat the syrup, crème fraîche, sugar, eggs, ground
ginger and orange zest together. Add the melted butter and
stir until fully incorporated. Beat in the flour and baking
powder, until the mixture is smooth (the texture will be quite
runny). Fold in the chopped ginger.

Pour the mixture into the prepared pan and bake for about
1 hour, or until the loaf is risen and golden and a skewer
comes out clean when inserted into the centre.

Leave to cool in the pan for 30 minutes, and then turn
onto a wire rack and leave until cold. Serve immediately or
store in an airtight container.

Mocha Loaf

Makes 1 x 900 g/2 lb loaf
Preparation time 1½ hours, plus cooling
You will need a loaf pan with a 900 g/2 lb/8-cup
capacity, lightly buttered and base-lined with baking
parchment or greaseproof paper

150 g/5 oz/5 squares plain (semi-sweet) chocolate, chopped
250 g/9 oz/2¼ sticks butter
250 g/9 oz/1¼ cups caster (superfine) sugar
4 eggs, beaten
150 g/5 oz/1¼ cups self-raising flour
100 g/3½ oz/½ cup semolina
2 tablespoons ground coffee
1 tablespoon instant coffee
1 small hot espresso

Mocha was the world's first commercially produced coffee and came from the rugged southern tip of the Arabian Peninsula, which is now a part of the Republic of Yemen. Although accounts differ as to how and why, somewhere in the 1800s, the name became associated with a coffee and chocolate combo used in cakes and confectionery. But something that tastes so good is bound to have a little history, isn't it?

Preheat the oven to 180°C/350°F/Gas mark 4. Put the chocolate into a heatproof bowl and place over a saucepan of hot water, stirring occasionally until smooth. Remove from the pan.

Cream the butter and sugar together until light and fluffy. Add the eggs, a little at a time, stirring in between each addition, until the mixture is smooth and all the eggs have been incorporated. Stir in the flour and semolina. Add the melted chocolate and beat until smooth. Stir the ground coffee into the espresso and beat into the creamed mixture.

Spoon into the prepared pan and bake for about 1 hour 10 minutes, until firm and springy to the touch.

Remove from the oven and leave to cool in the pan for about 20 minutes. Turn onto a wire rack and leave until completely cold. Store in an airtight container.

Maple and Pecan Tea Bread

Makes 1 x 900 g/2 lb loaf
Preparation time 1 hour 40 minutes, plus cooling
You will need a loaf pan with a 900 g/2 lb/8-cup
capacity, lightly buttered and base-lined with baking
parchment or greaseproof paper

350 g/12 oz /3 cups self-raising flour
2 teaspoons baking powder
100 g/3½ oz/½ cup soft brown sugar
150 ml/5 fl oz/½ cup maple syrup
100 ml/3½ fl oz/½ cup milk
150 g/5 oz/1¼ cups pecans, roughly chopped

Here's another loaf for buttering. Toasting is totally
optional but I think works well.

Preheat the oven to 180°C/350°F/Gas mark 4. Sift the flour
and baking powder into a large bowl. Stir in the sugar.

Beat the maple syrup and milk together, and stir into
the flour. Add the pecans and stir until they are evenly
incorporated throughout the mixture.

Spoon into the prepared pan and bake for 1 hour 20
minutes, or until risen and golden and a skewer inserted into
the centre of the loaf comes out clean.

Leave to cool in the pan for 10 minutes or so, and then
turn onto a wire rack and leave until completely cold. Serve
in slices, generously buttered. Store in an airtight container.

Raspberry, White Chocolate and Almond Loaf

Makes 1 x 900 g/2 lb loaf
Preparation time 2¼ hours, including cooling
You will need a loaf pan with a 900 g/2 lb/8-cup
capacity, lightly buttered and base-lined with baking
parchment or greaseproof paper

250 g/9 oz/2¼ sticks butter
250 g/9 oz/1¼ cups caster (superfine) sugar
4 eggs, beaten
100 g/3½ oz/1 cup plain (all-purpose) flour
150 g/5 oz/1¼ cups ground almonds
grated zest and juice 1 lemon
150 g/5 oz/1¼ cups raspberries
150 g/5 oz/5 squares white chocolate, roughly chopped
icing (confectioners') sugar, for dusting

Jean Cazals (the brilliant photographer who took the lovely shots for this book) absolutely adored this cake. Seriously. I was tickled to bits and back, especially because he's a Frenchman who takes far more than a passing interest in good things to eat. It's a moist, seductive combination of ground almonds, white chocolate and fresh raspberries, and so irresistibly easy to make.

Preheat the oven to 180°C/350°F/Gas mark 4. In a large bowl, cream together the butter and sugar until light and fluffy. Beat in the eggs, a little at a time, until fully incorporated (add a little of the flour if the mixture seems to be curdling). Once the eggs have been added, stir in the remaining flour and the ground almonds and lemon zest and juice.

Spoon the mixture evenly into the prepared pan. Scatter over the raspberries and white chocolate. Bake for about 1 hour 10 minutes, but check after 1 hour. The loaf should be risen and golden and a skewer should come out clean when inserted into the centre.

Leave the loaf to cool in the pan for 30 minutes, and then turn onto a wire rack and leave until cold. Dust with icing (confectioners') sugar and serve immediately, or store in an airtight container.

Carrot, Walnut and Sultana (Golden Raisin) Loaf

Makes 1 x 900 g/2 lb loaf
Preparation time 1 hour 20 minutes, plus cooling
You will need a loaf pan with a 900 g/2 lb/8-cup capacity, lightly buttered and base-lined with baking parchment or greaseproof paper

200 g/7 fl oz/¾ cup sunflower (canola) oil
300 g/10 oz/1⅓ cups dark muscovado (dark brown) sugar
3 eggs
300 g/10 oz/2¼ cups self-raising flour
2 teaspoons ground cinnamon
100 g/3½ oz/½ cup sultanas (golden raisins)
300 g/10 oz (peeled weight) carrots, grated
grated zest 1 orange
100 g/3½ oz/1 cup walnuts, chopped

This big, bold gutsy cake seems made for the sort of picnic I love on those slightly chilly autumn days that were made for being in the fresh air. It was a favourite on lovely bracing walks with my sister-in-law, my young nephews and my own sons, rambling through the woods and grounds of a very beautiful English country house called Castle Howard. We would always finish by tucking into a mini-feast overlooking the lake, watching the swans as we munched through thick slices of this cake, washed down with hot coffee.

Preheat the oven to 180°C/350°F/Gas mark 4. In a large bowl, beat the sunflower oil and sugar with the eggs. Stir in the flour, cinnamon and sultanas (golden raisins). Add the carrot, orange zest and walnuts and beat well until everything is fully incorporated.

Pour the batter into the prepared pan and bake for 1 hour, or until a skewer inserted into the centre of the loaf comes out clean.

Leave to cool in the pan for 20 minutes, and then turn onto a cooling rack until completely cold. Store in an airtight container.

Coffee Bean Loaf

Makes 1 x 900 g/2 lb loaf
Preparation time 1 hour 20 minutes, plus cooling
You will need a loaf pan with a 900 g/2 lb/8-cup
capacity, lightly buttered and base-lined with baking
parchment or greaseproof paper

250 g/9 oz/2¼ sticks butter
250 g/9 oz/1¼ cups caster (superfine) sugar
4 eggs, beaten
250 g/9 oz/2¼ cups self-raising flour
100 g/3½ oz/¾ cup semolina
1 small espresso
2 tablespoons freshly ground coffee

If you like the texture that poppy seeds add to a
cake and you're a coffee addict like me, then you'll
love this loaf. I've added semolina, too, which gives
it a light crumbliness to complement the slight
crunch of the coffee beans. I sometimes serve the
cake drizzled with a coffee icing, but, personally,
I prefer it unadorned, cut into thin slices with my
mid-morning espresso.

Preheat the oven to 180°C/350°F/Gas mark 4. Cream the
butter and sugar together until light and fluffy. Add the eggs,
a little at a time, stirring in between each addition, until the
mixture is smooth and all the eggs have been incorporated.
Stir in the flour and the semolina, and then beat in the
espresso and ground coffee.

Spoon the mixture into the prepared pan and bake for
about 1 hour, or until golden and springy to the touch.
Remove from the oven and leave to cool in the pan for about
20 minutes. Turn onto a wire rack and leave until completely
cold. Store in an airtight container.

Spiced Apple and Raisin Loaf

Makes 1 x 900 g/2 lb loaf
Preparation time 1 hour 10 minutes, plus cooling
You will need a loaf pan with a 900 g/2 lb/8-cup
capacity, lightly buttered and base-lined with baking
parchment or greaseproof paper

320 g/11 oz/2¾ cups plain (all-purpose) flour
2 teaspoons baking powder
1 teaspoon ground cinnamon
100 g/3½ oz/½ cup caster (superfine) sugar
2 tablespoons black treacle (molasses)
300 ml/½ pint/1¼ cups milk
2 apples, chopped
100 g/3½ oz/⅔ cup raisins
100 g/3½ oz/⅔ cup pecan nuts

A classic fruit and nut combo that makes a simple
but special loaf, and another one that's just
wonderful toasted.

Preheat the oven to 180°C/350°F/Gas mark 4. Sift the
flour, baking powder and cinnamon into a large bowl. Stir
in the sugar.

Gently heat the treacle (molasses) and milk together
(this will make it easier to mix) and stir into the dry
ingredients until thoroughly mixed. Fold in the apples,
raisins and pecan nuts.

Pour the mixture into the prepared pan and bake for about
50 minutes, or until the loaf is risen and golden and a skewer
inserted into the centre comes out clean.

Leave to cool in the pan for 10 minutes or so, and then
turn onto a wire rack to cool completely. Store in an
airtight container.

Walnut Tea Bread

Makes 1 x 900 g/2 lb loaf
Preparation time 2½ hours, including cooling.
You will need a loaf pan with a 900 g/2 lb/8-cup capacity, lightly buttered and base-lined with baking parchment or greaseproof paper.

350 g/12 oz/3 cups self-raising flour
2 teaspoons baking powder
100 g/3½ oz/½ cup caster (superfine) sugar
100 g/3½ oz/1 cup walnuts, roughly chopped
300 ml/½ pint/1¼ cups milk
2 tablespoons golden (corn) syrup, slightly warmed

I love this bread at breakfast, hot from the toaster and thickly buttered. Always two slices, too. But then I let the dog drag me out for a long walk afterwards, so it works out almost the same as having fresh fruit and a bowl of low-fat yoghurt.

Preheat the oven to 180°C/350°F/Gas mark 4. Sift the flour and baking powder together into a large bowl. Stir in the caster (superfine) sugar, and then the walnuts.

Beat the milk and warmed golden (corn) syrup together (warming the syrup will make it easier to mix). Stir into the dry ingredients until thoroughly incorporated.

Spoon the mixture into the prepared pan and bake for about 1 hour 10 minutes, or until the loaf is risen and golden and a skewer inserted into the centre comes out clean.

Leave the loaf to cool in the pan for 15 minutes or so, and then turn onto a wire rack and leave until completely cold. Serve with butter. Store in an airtight container.

Lavender and Orange Loaf

Makes 1x 450 g/1 lb loaf
Preparation time 1 hour 10 minutes, plus cooling
You will need a loaf pan with a 450 g/1 lb/4-cup capacity, lightly buttered and base-lined with baking parchment or greaseproof paper

100 g/3½ oz/½ cup butter
150 g/5 oz/¾ cup caster (superfine) sugar
2 eggs, beaten
150 g/5 oz/1¼ cups plain (all-purpose) flour
100 g/3½ oz/½ cup thick yoghurt
grated zest 1 orange
1 teaspoon dried lavender flowers
icing (confectioners') sugar, for dusting

Dried lavender flowers add a subtle but instantly recognizable flavour and aroma to this lovely cake. Serve it with a generous dredging of icing (confectioners') sugar and a cup of Earl Grey tea. A word of warning though: please don't be tempted to throw in a few extra lavender flowers to the mix; the cake will smell like pot pourri and rather than wanting to eat it, you may find it more suitable to use as a room freshener.

Preheat the oven to 180°C/350°F/Gas mark 4.

Cream the butter and sugar together in a large bowl until light and fluffy.

Beat in the eggs, a little at a time, until fully incorporated (add a little of the flour if the mixture seems to be curdling). Once the eggs have been added, stir in the remaining flour and then beat in the yoghurt until the mixture is smooth. Stir in the orange zest and lavender flowers.

Spoon the mixture evenly into the prepared pan. Bake for about 45–50 minutes, or until the cake is firm and golden and a skewer comes out clean when inserted into the centre.

Leave to cool in the pan for 20 minutes, and then turn onto a wire rack and leave until cold. Dust with icing (confectioners') sugar and serve immediately, or store in an airtight container.

Honey and Pecan loaf

Makes 1 x 900 g/2 lb loaf
Preparation time 2½ hours, including cooking, cooling
and drizzling
You will need a loaf pan with a 900 g/2 lb /8-cup
capacity, lightly buttered and base-lined with
baking parchment or greaseproof paper

350 g/12 oz/3 cups self-raising flour
2 teaspoons baking powder
100 g/3½ oz/½ cup caster (superfine) sugar
150 g/5 oz/1¼ cups pecan nuts, coarsely chopped
300 ml/½ pint/1¼ cups milk
2 tablespoons clear (golden) honey, slightly warmed

topping
4 tablespoons clear (golden) honey

This lovely loaf freezes well, but if ever I make it with
the intention of freezing the whole loaf, I usually omit
the honey drizzle until the loaf is defrosted and I
want to serve it.

Preheat the oven to 180°C/350°F/Gas mark 4. Sift the flour
and baking powder together into a large bowl. Stir in the
caster (superfine) sugar, and then 100 g/3½ oz/scant 1 cup of
the pecan nuts. Beat the milk and honey together, and then
stir the milk mixture into the dry ingredients until
thoroughly incorporated.

   Spoon the mixture into the prepared pan and scatter over
the remaining pecans. Bake for about 1 hour, or until the
loaf is risen and golden and a skewer inserted into the centre
comes out clean.

   Leave the loaf to cool in the pan for 15 minutes or so, and
then turn onto a wire rack. Drizzle with honey and leave
until completely cold. Store in an airtight container.

Soured (Sour) Cream, Lemon and Cherry Loaf

Makes 1 x 450 g/1 lb loaf
Preparation time 1 hour, plus cooling
You will need a loaf pan with a 450 g/1 lb/4-cup
capacity, lightly buttered and base-lined with baking
parchment or greaseproof paper

100 g/3½ oz/1 stick butter
175 g/6 oz/¾ cup caster (superfine) sugar
2 eggs, beaten
175 g/6 oz/1½ cups self-raising flour
100 ml/3½ fl oz/½ cup soured (sour) cream
juice and zest 1 lemon
100 g/3½ oz dried cherries

Chewy dried cherries in a lemony sour cream sponge
make this pretty bread perfect to serve in delicate
slices with a pot of tea.

Preheat the oven to 180°C/350°F/Gas mark 4. Beat the
butter and sugar together until light and fluffy. Beat in the
eggs, a little at a time until fully incorporated. You may need
to add a little of the flour to prevent the mixture curdling.
Once all the eggs have been incorporated, add the remaining
flour. Beat in the soured cream, lemon juice and zest, and
then the cherries.

   Spoon the mixture into the prepared pan and bake for
about 45 minutes, or until the loaf is risen and golden and
a skewer inserted into the centre comes out clean.

   Leave the loaf to cool in the pan for 20 minutes or so, and
then turn onto a wire rack and leave to cool completely.
Store in an airtight container.

Ginger Apple Sauce Loaf

Makes 1 x 900 g/2 lb loaf
Preparation time 1½ hours, plus cooling
You will need a loaf pan with a 900 g/2 lb/8-cup capacity, lightly buttered and base-lined with baking parchment or greaseproof paper.

320 g/11 oz/2¾ cups plain (all-purpose) flour
1 teaspoon bicarbonate of soda (baking soda)
2 teaspoons ground ginger
200 g/7 oz/1 cup caster (superfine) sugar
100 ml/3½ oz/⅓ cup clear (golden) honey
100 g/3½ oz/1 stick butter, melted
3 eggs, beaten
150 g/5 oz/½ cup sweetened chunky apple sauce

In England, apple sauce is something generally served as an accompaniment to roast pork. And to think a whole country could be missing out on discovering what a great addition it makes to ginger cake. Of course, you could make your own apple sauce, but a using a good-quality jar of chunky, slightly sweetened sauce is much quicker.

Preheat the oven to 180°C/350°F/Gas mark 4. Sift the flour and bicarbonate of soda (baking soda) together into a large bowl and stir in the ginger and caster (superfine) sugar.

Beat the honey, butter and eggs with the apple sauce. Stir into the dry ingredients until thoroughly incorporated.

Spoon the mixture into the prepared pan and bake for about 1 hour 10 minutes, or until the loaf is risen and golden and a skewer inserted into the centre comes out clean.

Leave the loaf to cool in the pan for 15 minutes or so, and then turn onto a wire rack and leave until completely cold. Store in an airtight container.

Blueberry and Almond Bread

Makes 1 x 900 g/2 lb loaf
Preparation time 1½ hours, plus cooling
You will need a loaf pan with a 800 g/2 lb/8-cup capacity, lightly buttered and base-lined with baking parchment or greaseproof paper

250 g/9 oz/2¼ sticks butter
200 g/7 oz/1 cup caster (superfine) sugar
3 eggs, beaten
250 g/8 oz/2¼ cups self-raising flour
100 g/3½ oz/½ cup ground almonds
100 g/3½ oz dried blueberries
1 teaspoon almond essence

I'm a serial nibbler and I can't resist dried blueberries. When I make this lovely moist almond bread I always buy twice as many as I need to account for my habit. If you are similarly affected, I suggest you do the same. The chewy little nuggets should be speckled evenly throughout the cake, which is not easy to achieve at all if you've eaten half of them straight from the packet beforehand.

Preheat the oven to 180°C/350°F/Gas mark 4. Cream the butter and sugar together in a large bowl. Stir in the beaten eggs, a little at a time, until fully incorporated. Add the flour and ground almonds, and then stir in the blueberries and almond essence.

Spoon the mixture into the prepared pan and bake for about 1 hour 10 minutes, or until a skewer inserted into the centre of the bread comes out clean. Leave to cool in the pan for 10 minutes, and then turn on a wire rack and leave to cool completely. Store in an airtight container.

Streusel-topped Blueberry Loaf

Makes 1 x 900 g/2 lb loaf
Preparation time 1¼ hours, plus cooling
You will need a loaf pan with a 900 g/2 lb/8-cup
capacity, lightly buttered and base-lined with baking
parchment or greaseproof paper

320 g/11 oz/2¾ cups plain (all-purpose) flour
2 tablespoons baking powder
150 g/5 oz/¾ cup caster (superfine) sugar
2 eggs
200 g/7 fl oz/¾ cup milk
120 g/4 oz/1 stick butter, melted and cooled
150 g/5 oz/ ¼ cups fresh blueberries

topping
50 g/1¾ oz/½ cup plain (all-purpose) flour
30 g/1 oz/2 tablespoons butter
50 g/1¾ oz/¼ cup caster (superfine) sugar
2 tablespoons macadamia nuts, roughly chopped

Streusel is a delicious crumbly combination of nuts,
butter, sugar and flour that makes a great topping
for sweet loaves containing fresh fruit. Almonds or
hazelnuts work particularly well with blueberries,
but the best of the lot to me are crunchy, creamy
macadamia nuts.

Preheat the oven to 180°C/350°F/Gas mark 4. Sift the
flour and baking powder together into a large bowl. Stir in
the sugar.

In a separate bowl, whisk the eggs and milk with the
butter. Stir lightly but thoroughly into the flour mixture and
then gently fold in the blueberries, taking care not to over
mix. Spoon into the prepared pan.

To make the topping, in a clean bowl, rub the flour
and butter together until the mixture resembles fine
breadcrumbs. Stir in the sugar and nuts. Scatter evenly
across the blueberry batter.

Bake for about 45 minutes, or until golden and risen and
a skewer inserted into the centre comes out clean.

Leave the cake to cool in the pan for 15 minutes, and then
turn carefully onto a wire cooling rack, taking care that the
crumble topping doesn't fall off. Leave until completely cold
and store in an airtight container.

Traditional Fruit Tea Bread

Makes 1 x 900 g/2 lb loaf
Preparation time 1½ hours, plus overnight standing, and cooling
You will need a loaf pan with a 900 g/2 lb/8-cup capacity, lightly buttered and base-lined with baking parchment or greaseproof paper

350 g/12 oz/2 cups mixed dried fruit
300 ml/½ pint/1¼ cups freshly brewed hot
   Earl Grey tea
400 g/14 oz/3¾ cups self-raising flour
1 teaspoon baking powder
1 egg, beaten

Wales is a tiny treasure of a country tucked alongside the southwest side of England and although it spans little over 20,000 sq km (7,722 sq miles), it is a land of breathtaking scenery and cosmopolitan cities. It even has its own language, and its very own prince, of course. This fruity bread is based on the traditional Welsh loaf known as 'bara brith', which in that very unique Welsh language literally translates as 'speckled bread'. Vary the dried fruit to suit your tastes, but I like a simple mixture of sultanas (golden raisins) and raisins.

Put the mixed fruit into a roomy bowl and pour over the freshly-brewed tea. Cover and leave to stand for several hours, preferably overnight.

When you are ready to bake the loaf, preheat the oven to 180°C/350°F/Gas mark 4. Sift the flour and baking powder together and stir evenly into the soaked fruit. Beat in the egg.

Pour the mixture into the prepared pan and baked for about 1½ hours, or until a skewer comes out clean when inserted into the centre of the loaf.

Leave to cool in the pan for 10 minutes or so, and then turn onto a wire rack and leave until completely cold. Serve with good butter and a pot of tea. Store in an airtight container.

Honey and Pine Nut Loaf

Makes 1 x 900 g/1 lb loaf
Preparation time 2½ hours, including cooling.
You will need a loaf pan with a 900 g/2 lb/8-cup
capacity, lightly buttered and base-lined with baking
parchment or greaseproof paper.

350 g/12 oz/3 cups self-raising flour
2 teaspoons baking powder
100 g/3½ oz caster (superfine) sugar
100 g/3½ oz/1 cup pine nuts
300 ml/½ pint/1¼ cups milk
2 tablespoons clear (golden) honey, slightly warmed

Here's another moist and delicious loaf that is best
served buttered, but as there is no fat in the batter,
you can indulge without guilt.

Preheat the oven to 180°C/350°F/Gas mark 4. Sift the flour
and baking powder together into a large bowl. Stir in the
caster (superfine) sugar, and then the pine nuts.

Beat the milk and warmed honey together (warm honey
will mix much more easily). Stir into the dry ingredients
until thoroughly incorporated.

Spoon the mixture into the prepared pan and bake for
about 1 hour, or until the loaf is risen and golden and a
skewer inserted into the centre comes out clean.

Leave the loaf to cool in the pan for 15 minutes or so, and
then turn onto a wire rack and leave until completely cold.
Serve with butter. Store in an airtight container

Ginger, Honey and Banana Bread

Makes 1 x 900 g/2 lb loaf
Preparation time 1¾ hours, plus cooling
You will need a loaf pan with a 900 g/2 lb/8-cup
capacity, lightly buttered and base-lined with baking
parchment or greaseproof paper

120 g/4 oz/1 stick butter
100 g/3½ oz/½ cup caster (superfine) sugar
4 tablespoons clear (golden) honey
2 eggs, beaten
250 g/9 oz/2¼ cups self-raising flour
2 bananas, mashed
100 g/3½ oz crystallized ginger, roughly chopped

This is another recipe where the ripeness of the
bananas is paramount to the success of the loaf
(see Banana and Chocolate Chip loaf, page 9).
Black bananas will give a fragrant, flavoursome cake;
under-ripe bananas will leave you never quite being
able to guess just what the cake is supposed to taste
of. I always keep some frozen black bananas to hand.
They can be used straight from the freezer not only
for some fabulous cakes, but for some pretty
impressive smoothies, too.

Preheat the oven to 180°C/350°F/Gas mark 4. In a large
bowl, cream together the butter and sugar until light and
fluffy. Beat in the honey. Add the eggs, a little at a time,
until fully incorporated (simply add a little of the flour if
the mixture seems to be curdling). Once the eggs have been
added, stir in the remaining flour, and then the mashed
bananas. Fold in the ginger until evenly mixed.

Spoon the mixture into the prepared pan. Bake for about
1 hour 20 minutes until risen and golden. A skewer should
come out clean when inserted into the centre of the loaf.

Leave to cool in the pan for 30 minutes, and then
turn onto a wire rack and leave until cold. Store in an
airtight container.

Pistachio, Cherry and Almond Loaf

Makes 1 x 450 g/1 lb loaf
Preparation time 1¼ hours plus cooling
You will need a loaf pan with a 450g/1lb 4cup
capacity, lightly buttered and base-lined with
baking parchment or greaseproof paper

250 g/9 oz/2¼ sticks butter
200 g/7 oz/1 cup caster (superfine) sugar
3 eggs, beaten
250 g/9 oz/2¼ cups self-raising flour
100 g/3½ oz/1 cup ground almonds
100 g/3½ oz dried cherries
100 g/3½ oz pistachios

Well, here's another recipe that features my favourite chewy dried cherries, this time with vibrant green pistachios dotted through a dense almond sponge. I like to think I have willpower, but give it to me with a nice pot of Earl Grey tea, and this is one of those loaves I usually sneak an extra slice of.

Preheat the oven to 180°C/350°F/Gas mark 4. Cream the butter and sugar together in a large bowl. Stir in the beaten eggs, a little at a time until fully incorporated. Add the flour and ground almonds, and then stir in the dried cherries and the pistachios.

Spoon the mixture into the prepared pan and bake for about 1 hour, or until a skewer inserted into the centre of the loaf comes out clean.

Leave to cool in the pan for 10 minutes or so, and then turn onto a wire rack and leave to cool completely. Store in an airtight container.

Glazed Tequila Loaf

Makes 1x 900 g/2 lb loaf
Preparation time 2¼ hours, including cooling
and glazing
You will need a loaf pan with a 900 g/2 lb/8-cup
capacity, lightly buttered and base-lined with baking
parchment or greaseproof paper

250 g/9 oz/1 cup butter
250 g/9 oz/1¼ cups caster (superfine) sugar
3 eggs, beaten
300 g/10 oz/2½ cups self-raising flour
grated zest and juice 2 limes

glaze
50 ml/1¾ fl oz/¼ cup tequila
grated zest and juice 2 limes
100 ml/3½ fl oz/½ cup water
200 g/7 oz/1 cup caster (superfine) sugar

The shiny glaze on this loaf has tequila in it. You don't
have to worry about getting tipsy after a slice or two,
but it does add a deliciously different element. If you
prefer not to use the tequila, simply use the juice of
an extra lime and a couple of tablespoons of
additional water. The loaf won't quite have the same
kick – but will still taste good.

Preheat the oven to 180°C/350°F/Gas mark 4. In a large
bowl, cream together the butter and sugar until light
and fluffy.

Beat in the eggs, a little at a time, until fully incorporated
(simply add a little of the flour if the mixture seems to be
curdling). Once the eggs have been added, stir in the
remaining flour, together with the lime zest and juice.

Spoon the mixture evenly into the prepared pan. Bake
for about 1 hour, or until the loaf is risen and golden and
a skewer comes out clean when inserted into the centre.

Leave to cool in the pan for 30 minutes, and then turn
onto a wire rack and leave until cold.

Place the tequila, lime juice and zest, water and caster
(superfine) sugar into a pan and bring to the boil. Stir until
the sugar has dissolved and the mixture has thickened and
is glossy. This should take 3 minutes or so. Leave to cool.
Remove the zest from the glaze and reserve. Drizzle the glaze
generously over the loaf. Decorate with the reserved zest and
serve immediately, or store in an airtight container.

Lemon, Almond and Polenta Loaf

Makes 1 x 900 g/2 lb loaf
Preparation time 1¼ hours, plus cooling
You will need a loaf pan with a 900 g/2 lb/8-cup capacity, lightly buttered and base-lined with baking parchment or greaseproof paper

250 g/9 oz/2¼ sticks butter
250 g/9 oz/1¼ cups caster (superfine) sugar
4 eggs, beaten
100 g/3½ oz/1 cup ground almonds
50 g/1¾ oz/½ cup plain (all-purpose) flour
100 g/3½ oz polenta
grated zest 2 lemons
juice 1 lemon

This is lemony, grainy and gorgeous. Loaf heaven.

Preheat the oven to 180°C/350°F/Gas mark 4. Cream the butter and sugar together in a large bowl. Stir in the eggs, a little at a time until fully incorporated. Add the flour, ground almonds and polenta, and beat until smooth. Stir in the lemon zest and juice, and beat well until fully incorporated.

Spoon the mixture into the prepared pan and bake for about 1 hour, or until a skewer inserted into the centre of the loaf comes out clean. Leave to cool in the pan for 10 minutes or so, and then turn onto a wire rack and leave to cool completely. Store in an airtight container.

Chocolate and Courgette (Zucchini) Loaf

Makes 2 x 450 g/1 lb loaves or 1 x 900 g/2 lb loaf
Preparation time 1 hour 25 minutes, plus cooling
You will need either 2 loaf pans, each with a 450 g/
1 lb/4-cup capacity or one 900 g/2 lb/8-cup capacity,
lightly buttered and base-lined with baking
parchment or greaseproof paper

250 g/9 oz/2¼ cups plain (all-purpose) flour
50 g/1¾ oz/⅓ cup (unsweetened) cocoa powder
1 teaspoon baking powder
1 teaspoon bicarbonate of soda (baking soda)
200 ml/7 fl oz/¾ cup sunflower (canola) oil
350 g/12 oz/1⅔ cups caster (superfine) sugar
3 eggs, beaten
200 g/7 oz/2 small courgettes (zucchini), grated

This loaf comes in 3D: dark, damp and dangerous.
Grated courgette (zucchini) adds a special sort of
texture and moistness that set off the chocolate
beautifully. I make two smaller loaves and freeze one,
although it never seems to be for very long.

Preheat the oven to 180°C/350°F/Gas mark 4. Sift the flour,
cocoa powder, baking powder and bicarbonate of soda into
a large bowl.

Beat the sunflower oil, caster (superfine) sugar and eggs
together until smooth. Stir into the dry ingredients and then
beat in the grated courgettes (zucchini).

Spoon the mixture into the prepared pan/s and bake for
about 1 hour if in two pans or 1 hour 15 minutes if in one
pan, or until the loaves are nicely risen and golden and
a skewer inserted into the centre comes out clean.

Leave the loaves to cool in the pan for 20 minutes or so,
and then turn onto a wire rack and leave to cool completely.
Store in an airtight container, or freeze.

Savoury Quick Breads

Courgette (Zucchini) and Cheddar Loaf

Makes 1 x 900 g/2 lb loaf
Preparation time 1½ hours, plus cooling
You will need a loaf pan with a 900 g/2 lb/8-cup
capacity, lightly buttered and base-lined with baking
parchment or greaseproof paper

320 g/11 oz/2¾ cups plain (all-purpose) flour
2 tablespoons baking powder
½ teaspoon salt
½ teaspoon coarsely cracked black pepper
120 g/4 oz/1 stick butter, melted
2 eggs, beaten
200 ml/7 fl oz/¾ cup whole milk
50 g/1¾ oz courgette (zucchini), grated
150 g/5 oz/1¼ cups mature (sharp) cheddar, grated

This pretty loaf, speckled with courgettes (zucchini)
is great served with soups. Use a good strong knock-
your-socks-off cheddar and the results will speak
for themselves.

Preheat the oven to 180°C/350°F/Gas mark 4. Sift the
flour, baking powder and salt into a large bowl. Stir in
the black pepper.

In a separate bowl, whisk the melted butter, eggs and
milk together, and then stir lightly but thoroughly into
the flour mix. Gently fold in the courgette (zucchini) and
100 g/3½ oz/1 cup of the grated cheese, until everything
is evenly incorporated. Take care not to over mix.

Spoon the mixture into the prepared pan and scatter
over the remaining cheese.

Bake for about 1 hour 10 minutes, or until the loaf is
nicely risen and golden and a skewer inserted into the
centre comes out clean.

Leave the loaf to cool in the pan for 20 minutes or so,
and then turn onto a wire rack and leave to cool completely.
Store in an airtight container.

Cheddar and Bacon Quick Bread

Makes 1 x 900 g/2 lb loaf
Preparation time 1 hour 20 minutes
You will need a loaf pan with a 900 g/2 lb/8-cup
capacity, lightly buttered and base-lined with baking
parchment or greaseproof paper

320 g/11 oz/2¾ cups plain (all-purpose) flour
2 tablespoons baking powder
½ teaspoon salt
½ teaspoon coarsely cracked black pepper
200 ml/7 fl oz/¾ cup sunflower (canola) oil
2 eggs, beaten
200 ml/7 fl oz whole milk
100 g/3½ oz/1 cup cheese, grated
100 g/3½ oz bacon lardons, lightly cooked
1 tablespoon wholegrain mustard

A lovely loaf to pop in a lunch box; my sons have a
soft spot for it.

Preheat the oven to 180°C/350°F/Gas mark 4. Sift the
flour, baking powder and salt into a large bowl and stir in
the black pepper.

In a separate bowl, whisk the sunflower oil, eggs and milk
together, and then stir lightly but thoroughly into the flour
mix. Fold in the cheese, the bacon lardons and mustard and
stir gently, until everything is evenly incorporated. Take care
not to over mix.

Spoon the mixture into the prepared pan and bake for
about 1 hour, or until the loaf is nicely risen and golden and
a skewer inserted into the centre comes out clean.

Leave the loaf to cool in the pan for 20 minutes or so,
and then turn onto a wire rack and leave to cool completely.
Store in an airtight container.

Basil and Sun-dried Tomato Bread

Makes 1 x 900 g/2 lb loaf
Preparation time 1 hour 20 minutes, plus cooling
You will need a loaf pan with a 900 g/2 lb/8-cup
capacity, lightly buttered and base-lined with baking
parchment or greaseproof paper

320 g/11 oz/2¾ cups plain (all-purpose) flour
2 tablespoons baking powder
½ teaspoon salt
½ teaspoon coarsely cracked black pepper
200 ml/7 fl oz/¾ cup sunflower (canola) oil
2 eggs, beaten
200 g/7 fl oz/¾ cup whole milk
100 g/3½ oz/1 cup Parmesan cheese, freshly grated
100 g/3½ oz sun-dried tomatoes, roughly chopped
large handful fresh basil, roughly torn

This loaf is so simple to make and yet oozes sunshine flavours. It makes a great alternative to bread with Mediterranean-style soups, especially a vibrant gazpacho, or a chunky minestrone. It's great with savoury butters too. I also find it dangerously addictive served with a salad of peppery watercress dotted with crumbly feta cheese.

Preheat the oven to 180°C/350°F/Gas mark 4. Sift the flour, baking powder and salt into a large bowl and stir in the black pepper.

In a separate bowl, whisk the sunflower oil, eggs and milk together, and then stir lightly but thoroughly into the flour mix. Fold in the Parmesan cheese, sun-dried tomatoes and basil until evenly incorporated. Take care not to over mix.

Spoon the mixture into the prepared pan and bake for about 1 hour, or until the loaf is nicely risen and golden and a skewer inserted into the centre comes out clean.

Leave the loaf to cool in the pan for 20 minutes or so, and then turn onto a wire rack and leave to cool completely. Store in an airtight container.

Blue Cheese, Fig and Walnut Bread

Makes 1 x 900 g/2 lb loaf
Preparation time 1¾ hours, including soaking,
plus cooling
You will need a loaf pan with a 900 g/2 lb/8-cup
capacity, lightly buttered and base-lined with baking
parchment or greaseproof paper

85 g/3 oz moist ready-to-eat figs
4 tablespoons Marsala
200 g/7 oz/1½ cups plain (all-purpose) flour
1 tablespoon baking powder
3 eggs, beaten
200 ml/7 fl oz/¾ cup soured (sour) cream or
  crème fraîche
175 g/6 oz/1½ cups strong blue cheese, crumbled
75 g/2½ oz/¾ cups walnuts, roughly chopped

Friends have described this lovely loaf as 'almost a meal in itself'. It's delicious with a simple spinach salad or peppery soup. Roquefort, mature Stilton and Gorgonzola are all favourite blue cheeses to use, but you may have others. Just remember to use one that has plenty of oomph…

Preheat the oven to 180°C/350°F/Gas mark 4. Cut the figs into pieces (about the same size as chubby raisins) and place them into a small bowl. Add the Marsala and leave to soak for 30 minutes or so.

Sift the flour and baking powder into a large bowl. In a separate bowl, beat the eggs and soured cream (or crème fraîche) together until smooth and stir into the flour until everything is well combined. Season with a little salt and a good grinding of black pepper, and add 150 g/5 oz/1¼ cups of the cheese, the figs, the Marsala in which they have been soaking, and all but a few walnuts.

Turn the mixture into the prepared pan. Scatter the remaining cheese and walnuts evenly over the top of the loaf. Bake for about 1 hour, until the loaf is golden brown and a skewer pushed into the centre comes out clean. Cool slightly in the pan, and then turn the loaf onto a wire rack to cool completely. Store in an airtight container.

Easy Cheesy Sweetcorn Loaf

Makes 1 x 450 g/1 lb loaf
Preparation time 1 hour 20 minutes, plus cooling
You will need a loaf pan with a 450 g/1 lb/4-cup capacity, lightly buttered and base-lined with baking parchment or greaseproof paper

100 g/3½ oz/1 cup plain (all-purpose) flour
100 g/3½ oz/½ cup semolina
1 teaspoon baking powder
salt and freshly ground black pepper
100 ml/3½ fl oz/½ cup milk
2 eggs, beaten
50 g/1¾ oz/½ stick butter, melted and cooled
100 g/3½ oz/½ cup frozen sweetcorn, thawed
100 g/3½ oz/1 cup cheddar cheese, grated

This is a favourite with children, probably because the naturally sweet flavour of the corn combines well with cheese, and the semolina gives it a lovely crumbly texture. A great loaf to pack into lunch boxes.

Preheat the oven to 180°C/350°F/Gas mark 4. In a large bowl, mix together the flour, semolina, baking powder, salt and black pepper.

In a separate bowl, whisk the milk, eggs and butter together. Stir into the dry ingredients until smooth, and then add the sweetcorn and cheese.

Spoon the mixture into the prepared pan. Bake for 1 hour, or until golden and risen and a skewer comes out clean when inserted into the centre of the loaf.

Leave to cool in the pan for 10 minutes or so, and then turn onto a wire rack until cold. Store in an airtight container.

Sunflower, Sesame and Pumpkin Seed Loaf

Makes 1 loaf
Preparation time 1 hour plus cooling
You will need a lightly buttered baking sheet

250 g/8 oz/2¼ cups plain (all-purpose) flour
250 g/8 oz/2¼ cups wholemeal (whole-wheat) flour
2 teaspoons bicarbonate of soda (baking soda)
1 teaspoon salt
1 tablespoon sunflower seeds
1 tablespoon sesame seeds
1 tablespoon pumpkin seeds
400 ml/14 fl oz/1¾ cups buttermilk

A delicious nutty variation on classic Irish soda bread. I use a combination of white and wholemeal flours for a good flavour without creating a loaf that is heavy enough to be used as an offensive weapon.

Preheat the oven to 220°C/450°F/Gas mark 7. Mix the flour and bicarbonate of soda together in a large bowl. Stir in the salt and seeds, then the buttermilk and mix to a smooth, soft dough. Knead the dough very lightly and form into a large round.

Transfer the loaf to a baking sheet and slash the bread in a cross shape that reaches from edge to edge. Bake for 20 minutes, and then reduce the oven temperature to 180°C/350°F/Gas mark 4 and bake for another 20 minutes until cooked. To test the bread, carefully lift up the bread and tap the bottom; it will sound hollow if the bread is cooked.

This loaf is best eaten warm straight from the oven, but is equally nice if left to cool and toasted before eating. Store in an airtight container.

Tri-colour Pesto and
Tomato Bread

Makes 1 x 900 g/2 lb loaf
Preparation time 1½ hours, plus cooling
You will need a loaf pan with a 900 g/2 lb/8-cup
capacity, lightly buttered and base-lined with baking
parchment or greaseproof paper

300 g/10 oz/2½ cups plain (all-purpose) flour
2 tablespoons baking powder
salt and freshly ground black pepper
100 ml/3½ fl oz/1 cup sunflower (canola) oil
2 eggs
200 ml/7 fl oz/1 cup milk
3 tablespoons sun-dried tomato paste (purée)
3 tablespoons good quality pesto
2 tablespoons grated Parmesan cheese

This is one of my favourite picnic breads. It's bliss
eaten outdoors with a roasted vegetable salad (and
a generous portion of sunshine). It is also really good
with Parmesan butter. To make this, add a little grated
Parmesan and a grinding of black pepper to some
butter and beat everything together until smooth,
then it keep in the fridge or freezer until needed.

When making this recipe, bear in mind that good
quality pesto is essential for both flavour and colour.
Home made is best. Simply whiz a generous handful
or two of fresh basil in a blender with a tablespoon of
pine nuts, a couple of cloves of garlic, some grated
Parmesan, a squeeze of lemon juice and enough olive
oil to create a coarsely-textured paste; tinker a little
until it tastes just right – and there you have it.

Preheat the oven to 180°C/350°F/Gas mark 4.

Sift the flour and baking powder into a large bowl and stir
in the salt and black pepper.

Whisk the sunflower oil, eggs and milk together in a
separate bowl, and then stir lightly but thoroughly into the
flour mix.

Spoon half of the mixture into a clean bowl.

Carefully fold the sun-dried tomato paste into the mixture
in one of the bowls, creating a rippled effect. Do the same
with the pesto and the other half of the mixture.

Spoon both the mixtures alternately into the prepared pan,
as if you were making a marble cake.

Turn a skewer gently through the two mixtures just to
swirl them together a little. Scatter over the cheese and bake
for about one hour and 10 minutes, or until the loaf is nicely
risen and golden and a skewer inserted into the centre comes
out clean.

Leave the loaf to cool in the pan for 10 minutes or so, and
then turn onto a wire rack and leave to cool completely.
Serve immediately or store in an airtight container.

Butternut Squash and Fennel Seed Bread

Makes 1 x 900 g/2 lb loaf
Preparation time 1½ hours, plus cooling
You will need a loaf pan with a 900 g/2 lb/8-cup capacity, lightly buttered and base-lined with baking parchment or greaseproof paper

300 g/10 oz/2½ cups self-raising flour
2 teaspoons baking powder
salt and freshly ground black pepper
100 g/3½ oz/1 stick butter, melted
2 eggs, beaten
200 ml/7 fl oz/¾ cup milk
200 g/7 oz butternut squash, peeled, deseeded and grated
1 tablespoon dried fennel seeds

Grated butternut squash makes the prettiest, tastiest sort of loaf you can imagine, especially with an added freckling of fennel seeds. A great bread to serve with soups; I love it with a bowl of beef chilli, too.

Preheat the oven to 180°C/350°F/Gas mark 4. Sift the flour, baking powder and salt into a large bowl and stir in the black pepper.

In a separate bowl, whisk the melted butter, eggs and milk together, and then stir lightly but thoroughly into the flour mix. Gently stir in the squash and the fennel seeds, taking care not to over mix.

Spoon the mixture into the prepared pan and bake for about 1 hour 10 minutes, or until the loaf is nicely risen and golden and a skewer inserted into the centre comes out clean. Leave the loaf to cool in the pan for 20 minutes or so, and then turn onto a wire rack and leave to cool completely. Store in an airtight container

Irish Soda Bread

Makes 1 loaf
Preparation time 1 hour
You will need a lightly buttered baking sheet

250 g/9 oz/2¼ cups wholemeal (whole-wheat) flour
250 g/9 oz/2¼ cups plain (all-purpose) flour
2 teaspoons bicarbonate of soda (baking soda)
1 teaspoon salt
400 ml/14 fl oz/1¾ cups buttermilk

Classic Irish soda bread can be an indispensable store-cupboard standby. I've made it before using milk that has been soured by squeezing in the juice of a lemon. The results aren't quite as good as buttermilk, but incredibly handy in an emergency.

Preheat the oven to 220°C/450°F/Gas mark 7. Mix the flours and bicarbonate of soda together in a large bowl. Stir in the salt, and then add the buttermilk and mix to a smooth, soft dough. Knead the dough very lightly and form into a large round.

Transfer the bread to a baking sheet and slash the bread in a cross shape that reaches from edge to edge. Bake for 20 minutes, and then reduce the oven temperature to 180°C/375°F/Gas mark 4 and bake for a further 20 minutes until golden and cooked. To test the bread, carefully lift up the bread and tap the bottom. It will sound hollow if the bread is cooked. This loaf is best eaten warm. Store in an airtight container.

Leek, Pancetta and Black Pepper Bread

Makes 1 x 900 g/2 lb loaf
Preparation time 1 hour 20 minutes, plus cooling
You will need a loaf pan with a 900 g/2 lb/8-cup
capacity, lightly buttered and base-lined with baking
parchment or greaseproof paper

320 g/11 oz/2¾ cups plain (all-purpose) flour
2 tablespoons baking powder
½ teaspoon salt
1 teaspoon coarsely cracked black pepper
120 g/4 oz/1 stick butter, melted
2 eggs, beaten
200 ml/7 fl oz/¾ cup whole milk
1 leek, roughly chopped
150 g/5 oz pancetta lardons, cooked

Tomato soup just isn't the same without a slice
or two of this tasty loaf, served warm with heaps
of tangy mustard butter. Simply beat your favourite
wholegrain mustard into good-quality butter, form it
into a log and wrap well in clingfilm (plastic wrap).
Keep it in the freezer until you want to use it, and
then cut off slices and bring to room temperature.
In fact, the loaf itself freezes beautifully, too (as with
most in the book). Packed in slices between layers
of greaseproof or parchment paper, you can remove
a slice at a time as you fancy it, and warm it through
in a low oven or pop it in the microwave for a
few seconds.

Preheat the oven to 180°C/350°F/Gas mark 4. Sift the
flour, baking powder and salt into a large bowl. Stir in the
black pepper.

In a separate bowl, whisk the melted butter with the eggs
and milk. Stir lightly but thoroughly into the flour mix.
Gently stir in the chopped leek and pancetta lardons until
thoroughly incorporated.

Spoon the mixture into the prepared pan and bake for
about 1 hour, or until the loaf is nicely risen and golden
and a skewer inserted into the centre comes out clean.

Leave the loaf to cool in the pan for 20 minutes or so,
and then turn onto a wire rack and leave to cool completely.
Store in an airtight container.

Crunchy Peanut Butter Loaf

Makes a 450 g/1 lb loaf
Preparation time: 1 hour and 20 minutes, plus cooling
You will need a 450 g /1 lb loaf pan, lightly buttered
and base-lined with some baking parchment or
greaseproof paper

250 g/9 oz/2 cups plain (all-purpose) flour
2 tablespoons baking powder
85 g/3 oz/⅓ cup crunchy peanut butter
85 g/3 oz/⅓ cup golden caster (superfine) sugar
300 ml/½ pint whole milk
100 g/3½ oz/⅔ cup roasted peanuts, roughly chopped
½ teaspoon cracked black pepper

This tasty loaf always reminds me of the outdoors –
it's perfect for picnics and even better topped with
cream cheese and chopped celery. Try it back at home,
cut into fingers and dunked into soft-boiled eggs.

Preheat the oven to 180°C/350°F/Gas mark 4.

Sieve the flour and baking powder together. In a separate
bowl, beat together the peanut butter, sugar and milk. Stir
this into the dry ingredients, and then add the roughly
chopped peanuts and the black pepper.

Spoon the mixture into the prepared pan and bake for
1 hour, until golden and risen and a skewer comes out clean
when inserted into the centre of the loaf.

Leave to cool in the pan for 10 minutes or so, and then
turn out onto a wire rack to cool completely. Store in an
airtight container, or freeze in slices.

Sweet Potato and Chilli Bread

Makes 1 x 900 g/2 lb loaf
Preparation time 2½hours, including cooling
You will need a loaf pan with a 900 g/2 lb/8 cup
capacity, lightly buttered and base-lined with baking
parchment or greaseproof paper

320 g/11 oz/2¾ cups plain (all-purpose) flour
1 teaspoon bicarbonate of soda (baking soda)
2 teaspoons ground ginger
salt and freshly ground black pepper
1 tablespoon black treacle (molasses), warmed
100 g/3½ oz/1 stick butter, melted
3 eggs, beaten
150 g/5 oz cooked sweet potato, puréed
2 tablespoons sweet chilli sauce
pinch dried chilli flakes

Unusual but definitely delicious, the sweet potato in this recipe gives the loaf a lovely dense, chewy texture. Pumpkin or butternut squash make fabulous substitutes. Add chilli to suit your own taste – it does complement the sweet potato incredibly well.

Preheat the oven to 180°C/350°F/Gas mark 4. Sift the flour, bicarbonate of soda, ginger and salt together into a large bowl. Stir in a little black pepper.

Beat the treacle (molasses), butter and eggs with the sweet potato purée. Stir into the dry ingredients until thoroughly incorporated. Stir in the chilli sauce and chilli flakes.

Spoon the mixture into the prepared pan and bake for about 1 hour 10 minutes, or until the loaf is risen and golden and a skewer inserted into the centre comes out clean.

Leave the loaf to cool in the pan for 15 minutes or so, and then turn onto a wire rack and leave until completely cold. Store in an airtight container.

Cheddar and Chive Muffin Bread

Makes 1 x 900 g/2 lb loaf
Preparation time 1 hour 20 minutes, plus cooling
You will need a loaf pan with a 900 g/2 lb/8-cup
capacity, lightly buttered and base-lined with baking
parchment or greaseproof paper

320 g/11 oz/2¾ cups plain (all-purpose) flour
2 tablespoons baking powder
½ teaspoon salt
½ teaspoon coarsely cracked black pepper
120 g/4 oz/1 stick butter, melted
2 eggs, beaten
200 ml/7 fl oz/¾ cup whole milk
2 tablespoon chopped fresh chives
150 g/5 oz/1¼ cups mature (sharp)
    cheddar cheese, grated

Cheese and chives are one of those classic, timeless combinations that will always work well. Simple but tasty, this bread is popular with all ages.

Preheat the oven to 180°C/350°F/Gas mark 4. Sift the flour, baking powder and salt into a large bowl and stir in the black pepper.

In a separate bowl, whisk the melted butter, eggs and milk together and then stir lightly but thoroughly into the flour mix. Gently stir in the chives and 100 g/3½ oz/1 cup of the cheese, taking care not to over mix.

Spoon the mixture into the prepared pan and scatter over the remaining grated cheese. Bake for about 1 hour, or until the loaf is nicely risen and golden and a skewer inserted into the centre comes out clean.

Leave the loaf to cool in the pan for 20 minutes or so, and then turn onto a wire rack and leave to cool completely. Store in an airtight container.

Gruyère and Toasted Pumpkin Seed Loaf

Makes 1 x 900 g/2 lb loaf
Preparation time 1 hour 20 minutes, plus cooling
You will need a loaf pan with a 900 g/2 lb/8-cup capacity, lightly buttered and base-lined with baking parchment or greaseproof paper

pumpkin seeds
2 tablespoons pumpkin seeds
2 teaspoons extra virgin olive oil
pinch salt

loaf
300 g/10 oz/2½ cups plain (all-purpose) flour
2 tablespoons baking powder
salt and freshly cracked black pepper
200 ml/7 fl oz/¾ cup milk
2 eggs, beaten
120 g/4 oz/1 cup Gruyère cheese, grated

I know I'm biased because it's my recipe – but the toasted pumpkin seeds taste fantastic in this bread. In fact, they taste pretty good hot off the tray too, so I suggest you take my advice and make extra for munching.

Preheat the oven to 180°C/350°F/Gas mark 4.
To toast the pumpkin seeds, mix the seeds, olive oil and salt together and spread on a baking tray in an even layer. Transfer to the oven and roast for 10 minutes or so until golden. Leave to cool.

To make the loaf, sift the flour, baking powder and salt into a large bowl and stir in the black pepper.

In a separate bowl, whisk the milk and eggs together, and then stir lightly but thoroughly into the flour mix. Stir in the cheese and the cooled pumpkin seeds, taking care not to over mix.

Spoon the mixture into the prepared pan and bake for about 1 hour, or until the loaf is nicely risen and golden and a skewer inserted into the middle of the loaf comes out clean.

Leave the loaf to cool in the pan for 20 minutes or so, and then turn onto a wire rack and leave to cool completely. Store in an airtight container.

Easy Olive and Parmesan Bread

Makes 1 x 900 g/2 lb loaf
Preparation time 1 hour 20 minutes, plus cooling
You will need a loaf pan with a 900 g/2 lb/8-cup
capacity, lightly buttered and base-lined with baking
parchment or greaseproof paper

320 g/11 oz/2¾ cups plain (all-purpose) flour
2 tablespoons baking powder
½ teaspoon coarsely cracked black pepper
100 g/3½ oz/1 cup Parmesan cheese, grated
50 g/2 oz butter, melted
50 ml/2 fl oz extra virgin olive oil
2 eggs, beaten
200 ml/7 fl oz/¾ cup whole milk
100 g/3½ oz pitted mixed olives, roughly chopped

All olives begin life green. As they ripen in the sun,
the sugar and acids they contain are transformed
into oil and the colour of the flesh turns from green
through purple to black. Green olives are the least
oily and will have a sharper flavour; black olives
contain a greater amount of oil and therefore have
a more mellow flavour. Using a combination of the
two for this loaf gives a balanced flavour and a lovely
appearance. But using exclusively green or black
would give delicious results, too.

Preheat the oven to 180°C/350°F/Gas mark 4. Sift the flour
and baking powder into a large bowl. Stir in the black pepper
and Parmesan cheese.

In a separate bowl, whisk the melted butter and olive oil
with the eggs and milk. Stir lightly but thoroughly into the
flour mix. Gently fold in the olives until evenly incorporated.
Take care not to over mix.

Spoon the mixture into the prepared pan and bake for
about 1 hour, or until the loaf is nicely risen and golden and
a skewer inserted into the centre comes out clean.

Leave the loaf to cool in the pan for 20 minutes or so,
and then turn onto a wire rack and leave to cool. Store in an
airtight container.

Chilli and Goats' Cheese Bread

Makes 1 loaf
Preparation time 1 hour
You will need a lightly buttered baking sheet

500 g/1 lb 2 oz/4½ cups plain (all-purpose) flour
2 teaspoons bicarbonate of soda (baking soda)
1 teaspoon salt
1 teaspoon freshly cracked black pepper
150 g/5 oz/1¼ cups goats' cheese, finely crumbled
2 chillies, deseeded and finely chopped
400 ml/14 fl oz/1¾ cups buttermilk

This is another easy-peasy recipe from the soda bread camp. I often substitute chopped spring onions (scallions) for the chilli. I have also been known to throw caution to the wind and add both.

Preheat the oven to 220°C/450°F/Gas mark 8. Mix the flour and bicarbonate of soda together in a large bowl. Stir in the salt and pepper, and then add the cheese and chillies. Add the buttermilk and mix to a smooth, soft dough. Knead the dough very lightly and form into a large round. Transfer to a baking tray and slash the bread in a cross shape that reaches from edge to edge.

Bake the bread for 20 minutes, and then reduce the oven temperature to 180°C/375°F/Gas mark 5 and cook for another 20 minutes until cooked. To test the bread, carefully lift it up and tap the bottom; it will sound hollow if the bread is cooked. This loaf is best eaten warm straight from the oven, but is equally as nice if left to cool and toasted before eating. Store in an airtight container.

Spiced Chorizo and Herb Quick bread

Makes 1 x 900 g/2 lb loaf
Preparation time 1 hour 20 minutes, plus cooling
You will need a loaf pan with a 900 g/2 lb/8-cup
capacity, lightly buttered and base-lined with baking
parchment or greaseproof paper

320 g/11 oz/2¾ cups plain (all-purpose) flour
2 tablespoons baking powder
1 teaspoon garlic salt (optional)
1 teaspoon freshly cracked black pepper
2 teaspoons dried mixed herbs
1 teaspoon chilli flakes (optional)
120 g/4 oz/1 stick butter, melted
2 eggs
200 ml/7 fl oz/¾ cup milk
2 tablespoons tomato ketchup
150 g/5 oz chorizo, roughly diced

Choose a good-quality chorizo that isn't too fatty
or gristly.

Preheat the oven to 180°C/350°F/Gas mark 4. Sift the flour
and baking powder into a large bowl and stir in the garlic salt
(if using), black pepper, dried herbs and chilli flakes (if using).

In a separate bowl, whisk the melted butter, eggs, milk and
tomato ketchup together. Stir lightly but thoroughly into the
flour mix. Fold in all but a scant tablespoon of the chorizo.

Spoon into the prepared pan and scatter the remaining
chorizo over the top. Bake for about 1 hour 10 minutes, or
until the loaf is nicely risen and golden and a skewer inserted
into the middle comes out clean.

Leave the loaf to cool in the pan for 20 minutes or so, and
then turn onto a wire rack and leave to cool completely.
Store in an airtight container.

Feta and Sun-dried Pepper Bread

Makes 1 x 900 g/2 lb loaf
Preparation time 1½ hours, plus cooling
You will need a loaf pan with a 900 g/2 lb/8-cup
capacity, lightly buttered and base-lined with baking
parchment or greaseproof paper

300 g/10 oz/2½ cups plain (all-purpose) flour
2 tablespoons baking powder
salt and freshly ground black pepper
100 ml/3½ fl oz/½ cup extra virgin olive oil (or olive oil
    and drained sun-dried pepper oil combined)
2 eggs, beaten
200 ml/7 fl oz/¾ cup milk
200 g/7 oz/1¾ cups feta, finely crumbled
200 g/7 oz sun-dried peppers in olive oil, drained and
    roughly chopped

This bread contains two of my favourite ingredients,
so it's not surprising that the bread itself figures
high on my list. Sun-dried peppers have a more
concentrated flavour than peppers that have simply
been roasted. For a loaf with extra flavour, use any oil
you drain from the peppers towards making up the
quantity of olive oil specified in the recipe.

Preheat the oven to 180°C/350°F/Gas mark 4. Sift the
flour, baking powder and salt into a large bowl and stir in
the black pepper.

In a separate bowl, whisk the olive oil (or combined oils),
eggs and milk together and then stir lightly but thoroughly
into the flour mix. Fold in the feta cheese and sun-dried
peppers, taking care not to over mix.

Spoon the mixture into the prepared pan and bake for
about 1 hour 10 minutes, or until the loaf is nicely risen and
golden and a skewer inserted into the centre comes out clean.

Leave the loaf to cool in the pan for 10 minutes or so, and
then turn onto a wire rack and leave to cool completely.
Store in an airtight container.

Quick Parmesan and Polenta Bread

Makes 1 x 900 g/2 lb loaf
Preparation time 1 hour 10 minutes, plus cooling
You will need a loaf pan with a 900 g/2 lb/8-cup
capacity, lightly buttered and base-lined with baking
parchment or greaseproof paper

200 g/7 oz/1¾ cups plain (all-purpose) flour
2 tablespoons baking powder
100 g/3½ oz/¾ cup polenta
freshly ground black pepper
100 ml/3½ fl oz/½ cup olive oil
2 eggs
200 ml/7 fl oz/31 cup milk
120 g/4 oz/1 cup Parmesan cheese, grated

This is lovely in a lunch box, with a cold pasta salad.
Occasionally, I've cut a left-over slice or two into small
chunks and baked them until crisp in the oven, to
serve as little croutons with creamy tomato soup.

Preheat the oven to 180°C/350°F/Gas mark 4. Sift the flour
and baking powder into a large bowl and stir in the polenta
and black pepper.

In a separate bowl, whisk the olive oil, eggs and milk
together, and then stir lightly but thoroughly into the
flour mix. Gently fold in the Parmesan, taking care not to
over mix.

Spoon the mixture into the prepared pan and bake for
about 50 minutes, or until the loaf is nicely risen and golden
and a skewer inserted into the centre comes out clean.

Leave the loaf to cool in the pan for 20 minutes or so, and
then turn onto a wire rack and leave to cool completely.
Store in an airtight container.

Manchego Cheese, Caper and Sunflower Seed Soda Bread

Makes 1 loaf
Preparation time 1 hour
You will need a lightly buttered baking sheet

500 g/1 lb 2 oz/4½ cups plain (all-purpose) flour
2 teaspoons bicarbonate of soda (baking soda)
1 teaspoon salt
100 g/3½ oz/1 cup Manchego cheese, grated
2 tablespoons capers, rinsed, dried and roughly chopped
50 g/2 oz/½ cup sunflower seeds
400 ml/14 fl oz/1¾ cups buttermilk

Manchego cheese, capers and sunflower seeds add fabulous punch to soda bread. Strong cheddar makes a good substitute for the Manchego.

Preheat the oven to 220°C/450°F/Gas mark 7. Mix the flour, baking soda and salt together in a large bowl. Stir in the cheese, capers and sunflower seeds and then add the buttermilk and mix to a smooth, soft dough. Knead very lightly and form into a large round.

Transfer to a baking tray and slash the bread in a cross shape that reaches from edge to edge. Bake for 20 minutes, and then reduce the oven temperature to 180°C/375°F/Gas mark 4 and bake for another 20 minutes until cooked. To test the bread, carefully lift up the bread and tap the bottom; it will sound hollow if the bread is cooked. Store in an airtight container.

Savoury Carrot and Chilli Loaf

Makes 1 x 900 g/2 lb loaf
Preparation time 1 hour 20 minutes, plus cooling
You will need a loaf pan with a 900 g/2 lb/8-cup
capacity, lightly buttered and base-lined with baking
parchment or greaseproof paper

320 g/11 oz/2¾ cups plain (all-purpose) flour
2 tablespoons baking powder
½ teaspoon salt
½ teaspoon coarsely cracked black pepper
120 g/4 oz/1 stick butter, melted
2 eggs, beaten
200 g/7 fl oz/¾ cup whole milk
2 tablespoons wholegrain mustard
300 g/10 oz carrot, grated
bunch fresh thyme, leaves only
1 teaspoon dried chilli flakes (optional)

I love this bread. There's something about the combination of sweet, moist carrots and fragrant thyme that works beautifully together. Add wholegrain mustard and a little kick of chilli and you get heaven in a loaf pan.

Preheat the oven to 180°C/350°F/Gas mark 4. Sift the flour, baking powder and salt into a large bowl and stir in the black pepper.

In a separate bowl, whisk the melted butter, eggs, milk and mustard together, and then stir lightly but thoroughly into the flour mix. Gently stir in the carrot, thyme and chilli flakes, if using, taking care not to over mix. Spoon the mixture into the prepared pan and bake for about 1 hour, or until the loaf is nicely risen and golden and a skewer inserted into the centre comes out clean. Leave the loaf to cool in the pan for 20 minutes or so, and then turn out onto a wire rack and leave to cool completely.

Roasted Pepper Bread

Makes 1 x 900 g/2 lb loaf
Preparation time 1¾ hours, plus cooling
You will need a loaf pan with a 900 g/2 lb/8-cup
capacity, lightly buttered and base-lined with baking
parchment or greaseproof paper

2 red peppers
3 tablespoons olive oil
salt and freshly ground black pepper
300 g/10 oz/2½ cups plain (all-purpose) flour
2 tablespoons baking powder
100 ml/3½ fl oz/½ cup sunflower (canola) oil
2 eggs, beaten
200 ml/7 fl oz/¾ cup milk

I first made this bread to use up a couple of slightly
wizened red peppers and I liked it so much it stayed
in my repertoire. Because of the time involved
roasting the peppers, I tend to double the quantities
and make two loaves at a time and freeze one.

Preheat the oven to 200°C/400°F/Gas mark 6. Top and tail
the peppers, remove all the seeds and membrane and slice the
flesh into strips. Place the strips on a roasting tray, drizzle
over the olive oil, season with a little salt and freshly ground
black pepper, and then roast for about 15 minutes until soft.
Remove from the oven and leave to cool.
    Sift the flour and baking powder into a large bowl and stir
in a little salt and black pepper.
    In a separate bowl, whisk the sunflower oil, eggs, milk and
mustard together, and then stir lightly but thoroughly into
the flour mix. Fold in the roasted peppers, taking care not to
over mix.
    Spoon the mixture into the prepared pan and bake for
about 1 hour 10 minutes, or until the loaf is nicely risen and
golden and a skewer inserted into the centre comes out clean.
    Leave the loaf to cool in the pan for 20 minutes or so, and
then turn onto a wire rack and leave to cool completely.
Store in an airtight container.

Country Ham and Chive Bread

Makes 1 x 900 g/2 lb loaf
Preparation time 1 hour 20 minute, plus cooling
You will need a loaf pan with a 900 g/2 lb/8-cup
capacity, lightly buttered and base-lined with baking
parchment or greaseproof paper

300 g/10 oz/2½ cups plain (all-purpose) flour
2 tablespoons baking powder
salt and freshly ground black pepper
100 ml/3½ fl oz/½ cup olive oil
2 eggs
200 ml/7 fl oz/¾ cup milk
1 tablespoon wholegrain mustard
150 g/5 oz/1 cup cooked ham, diced
bunch fresh chives, finely chopped

Another classic partnership, ham and chives work
well together in this easy loaf. A good portion of fresh
air and a picnic blanket suits this bread well.

Preheat the oven to 180°C/350°F/Gas mark 4. Sift the flour
and baking powder into a large bowl and stir in a little salt
and finely ground black pepper.

In a separate bowl, whisk the olive oil, eggs, milk and
mustard together, and then stir lightly but thoroughly into
the flour mix. Gently fold in the ham and the chives, taking
care not to over mix.

Spoon the mixture into the prepared pan and bake for
about 1 hour, or until the loaf is nicely risen and golden and
a skewer inserted into the middle of the loaf comes out clean.

Leave the loaf to cool in the pan for 20 minutes or so, and
then turn onto a wire rack and leave to cool completely.
Store in an airtight container.

Sesame Loaf

Makes 1 x 450 g/1 lb loaf
Preparation time 1 hour 10 minutes, plus cooling
You will need a loaf pain with a 450 g/1 lb/4-cup
capacity, lightly buttered and base-lined with baking
parchment or greaseproof paper

120 g/4 oz/½ cup butter
120 g/4 oz/½ cup caster (superfine) sugar
2 eggs, beaten
120 g/4 oz/1 cup self-raising flour
50 g/1¾ oz sesame seeds

This loaf has a lovely crunchy texture and the
unmistakably delicious flavour of sesame seeds.
It may seem a little strange to see a loaf with sugar
in it make an appearance in the savoury section of
this book, but I love it best of all served with cream
cheese, crumbly feta, or even a salty Italian Gorgonzola.
Adding a sweet touch seems to highlight the flavour
of the sesame seeds so beautifully. That said, if you
prefer to serve it unadorned, then do so – I think
you'll be delighted with it either way.

Preheat the oven to 180°C/350 F/Gas mark 4.

Cream the butter and sugar together until light and fluffy.
Add the eggs, a little at a time, beating in between each
addition, until the mixture is smooth and all the eggs have
been incorporated. Stir in the flour and then beat in the
sesame seeds.

Spoon the mixture into the prepared pan and bake for
about 45–50 minutes, or until golden and springy to the
touch. Remove from the oven and leave to cool in the pan
for about 10 minutes before turning onto a wire rack.

Leave until completely cold, and then serve immediately
or store in an airtight container.

Rocket (Aragula) and Pecorino Bread

Makes 1 x 900 g/2 lb loaf
Preparation time 1¼ hours, plus cooling
You will need a loaf pan with a 900 g/2 lb/8-cup
capacity, lightly buttered and base-lined with baking
parchment or greaseproof paper

300 g/10 oz/2½ cups plain (all-purpose) flour
2 tablespoons baking powder
freshly ground black pepper
100 ml/3½ fl oz/½ cup olive oil
2 eggs, beaten
200 ml/7 fl oz/¾ cup milk
120 g/4 oz/1 cup pecorino cheese, grated
100 g/3½ oz rocket (arugula), roughly chopped

Peppery rocket (arugula) and salty pecorino make a
fabulous salad. The same combo makes a great quick
bread, too.

Preheat the oven to 180°C/350°F/Gas mark 4. Sift the
flour and baking powder into a large bowl and stir in
the black pepper.

In a separate bowl, whisk the olive oil, eggs and milk
together and then stir lightly but thoroughly into the flour
mix. Gently fold in the pecorino cheese and rocket (arugula),
taking care not to over mix.

Spoon the mixture into the prepared pan and bake for
about 1 hour, or until the loaf is nicely risen and golden and
a skewer inserted into the centre comes out clean.

Leave the loaf to cool in the pan for 20 minutes or so, and
then turn onto a wire rack and leave to cool completely.
Store in an airtight container.

Celebration Quick Breads

Peach Streusel Loaf

Makes 1 x 900 g/2 lb loaf
Preparation time 1¼ hours, plus cooling
You will need a loaf pan with a 900 g/2 lb/8-cup
capacity, lightly buttered and base-lined with baking
parchment or greaseproof paper

320 g/11 oz/2¾ cups plain (all-purpose) flour
2 tablespoons baking powder
150 g/5 oz/¾ cup caster (superfine) sugar
2 eggs
200 ml/7 fl oz/¾ cup milk
120 g/4 oz/1 stick butter, melted and cooled
1 ripe but firm peach, diced

topping
50 g/1¾ oz/½ cup plain (all-purpose) flour
30 g/1 oz/2 tablespoons butter
50 g/1¾ oz/¼ cup light muscovado (dark brown) sugar
2 tablespoons toasted hazelnuts, roughly chopped

Fresh peaches only have a short season but as this is
such a nice loaf try substituting dried peaches. Fresh
apples work well, too.

Preheat the oven to 180°C/350°F/Gas mark 4. Sift the
flour and baking powder together into a large bowl. Stir
in the sugar.

In a separate bowl, whisk the eggs and milk with the
butter. Stir lightly but thoroughly into the flour mixture
and then gently fold in the diced peach, taking care not to
over mix.

Spoon the mixture into the prepared pan.

To make the topping, in a clean bowl, rub the flour and
butter together until the butter is evenly incorporated. Stir in
the sugar and hazelnuts. Scatter evenly across the top of the
loaf batter in the pan. Bake for about 45 minutes, or until
golden and risen and a skewer inserted into the centre comes
out clean.

Leave the loaf to cool in the pan for 15 minutes, and then
turn out carefully onto a wire cooling rack, taking care that
the streusel topping doesn't fall off. Leave until completely
cold and store in an airtight container.

Cranberry and Almond Paste Loaf

Makes 1 x 900 g/2 lb loaf
Preparation time 1½ hours, plus cooling
You will need a loaf pan with a 900 g/2 lb/8-cup capacity, lightly buttered and base-lined with baking parchment or greaseproof paper

250 g/9 oz/2¼ sticks butter
250 g/9 oz/1¼ cups caster (superfine) sugar
4 eggs, beaten
150 g/5 oz/1¼ cups self-raising flour
100 g/3½ oz/1 cup ground almonds
50 g/1¾ oz marzipan (almond paste), grated
100 g/3½ oz dried cranberries
2 tablespoons flaked almonds

Here I am again, feeding my addiction for all things almond. I just love them in cakes – ground, flaked, whole, chopped and transformed into sweet almond paste or marzipan. This loaf tastes as good as it looks and to me is always a 'two-big-slices-then-power-walk-the-dog' sort of loaf.

Preheat the oven to 180°C/350°F/Gas mark 4. Cream the butter and sugar together until light and fluffy. Add the eggs, a little at a time, stirring well between each addition, until the mixture is smooth and all the eggs have been incorporated. Stir in the flour and ground almonds, and then fold in the grated almond paste and cranberries.

Spoon the mixture into the prepared pan and scatter over the flaked almonds. Bake for about 1 hour 10 minutes, or until golden and springy to the touch.

Remove from the oven and leave to cool in the pan for about 20 minutes. Turn onto a wire rack and leave until completely cold. Store in an airtight container.

Winter Spiced Loaf

Makes 1 x 900 g/2 lb loaf
Preparation time 1 hour 20 minutes, plus cooling
You will need a loaf pan with a 900 g/2 lb/8-cup capacity, lightly buttered and base-lined with baking parchment or greaseproof paper

320 g/11 oz/2¾ cups plain (all-purpose) flour
2 teaspoons bicarbonate of soda (baking soda)
2 teaspoons ground ginger
2 teaspoons ground cinnamon
175 g/6 oz/1½ sticks butter
100 ml/3½ fl oz/½ cup milk
250 ml/9 fl oz/1 cup soured (sour) cream
2 eggs, beaten
400 g/14 oz/2 cups dark muscovado (dark brown) sugar

Ginger, cinnamon and muscovado (dark brown) sugar make a dark tasty loaf, but soured (sour) cream helps give it a lovely, surprisingly light texture. This is another winter-walk loaf to have with a hot cup of tea.

Preheat the oven to 180°C/350°F/Gas mark 4. Sift the flour, bicarbonate of soda and spices into a large bowl.

Place the butter and milk into a saucepan and heat gently until the butter has melted. Pour into the flour mixture and stir well until thoroughly combined. Add the soured cream and eggs, stir in the sugar and beat until smooth.

Pour the batter into the prepared pan and bake for about 1 hour, or until the loaf is risen and golden and a skewer inserted into the centre comes out clean.

Leave the loaf to cool in the pan for 15 minutes or so, and then turn onto a wire rack and leave until completely cold. Store in an airtight container.

Apple and Pecan Loaf

Makes 1 x 900 g/2 lb loaf
Preparation time 1½ hours, plus cooling
You will need a loaf pan with a 900 g/2 lb/8-cup
capacity, lightly buttered and base-lined with baking
parchment or greaseproof paper

250 g/9 oz/2¼ sticks butter
300 g/10 oz/2½ cups self-raising flour
300 g/10 oz/1⅓ cups caster (superfine) sugar
150 g/5 oz/1¼ cups pecans, roughly chopped
3 apples, cored and coarsely chopped
2 eggs, beaten

I love apples and pecans together, and this is another
favourite for picnics and lunch boxes. Choose crunchy
well-flavoured dessert apples and leave the skin on –
doing so adds to the flavour, and the loaf looks much
prettier, too.

Preheat the oven to 180°C/350°F/Gas Mark 4. Rub the
butter and flour together until the mixture resembles fine
breadcrumbs. Stir in the sugar. Add the pecans and apples
and mix in thoroughly and evenly. Stir in the eggs. Spoon the
mixture into the prepared pan and bake for about 1 hour 10
minutes, or until a skewer inserted into the centre of the cake
comes out clean.

Leave to cool in the pan, and then turn out onto a wire
rack and leave to cool completely. Store in an airtight
container. This loaf freezes exceptionally well.

Cranberry and Pecan Bread

Makes 1 x 900 g/2 lb loaf
Preparation time 1 hour 20 minutes, plus cooling
You will need a loaf pan with a 900 g/2 lb/8-cup
capacity, lightly buttered and base-lined with baking
parchment or greaseproof paper.

350 g/12 oz/3 cups self-raising flour
2 teaspoons baking powder
100 g/3½ oz/½ cup caster (superfine) sugar
100 g/3½ oz dried cranberries
100 g/3½ g/1 cup walnuts, roughly chopped
300 ml/½ pint/1¼ cups milk
2 tablespoons golden (corn) syrup

Cranberries, like cherries, respond well to drying and
to me add a much livelier flavour to baking than the
more traditional fruits such as raisins and sultanas
(golden raisins). This is lovely served thinly sliced
and buttered.

Preheat the oven to 180°C/350°F/Gas mark 4. Sift the flour
and baking powder together into a large bowl. Stir in the
caster (superfine) sugar, cranberries and walnuts.

Heat the milk and warmed golden (corn) syrup together,
and stir into the dry ingredients until thoroughly incorporated.

Spoon the mixture into the prepared pan and bake for
about 1 hour, or until the loaf is risen and golden and a
skewer inserted into the centre comes out clean.

Leave the loaf to cool in the pan for 15 minutes or so, and
then turn onto a wire rack and leave until completely cold.
Store in an airtight container.

White Chocolate and Orange Bread

Makes 1 x 900 g/2 lb loaf
Preparation time 2¾ hours, including cooling
and icing
You will need a loaf pan with a 900 g/2 lb/8-cup
capacity, lightly buttered and base-lined with baking
parchment or greaseproof paper

320 g/11 oz/2¾ cups plain (all-purpose) flour
2 teaspoons baking powder
200 g/7 oz/1 cup caster (superfine) sugar
200 g/7 oz/7 squares white chocolate, chopped
100 ml/3½ fl oz/½ cup milk
100 g/3½ oz/1 stick butter, diced
grated zest and juice 1 large orange

topping
50 g/1¾ oz/2 squares white chocolate, melted
grated zest 1 small orange

I had originally intended to use dark chocolate in this recipe, but then had some lovely white chocolate left over from a tutored chocolate tasting I did at a charity dinner. Of course white chocolate isn't really 'chocolate' in the strictest sense because it doesn't contain cocoa solids but is made from just cocoa butter, sugar and milk. Nevertheless, it still tastes pretty special and makes a great match with oranges.

Preheat the oven to 180°C/350°F/Gas mark 4. Sift the flour and baking powder into a large bowl. Stir in the sugar.

Heat the white chocolate, milk and butter together until the chocolate and butter have melted. Stir into the dry ingredients until fully incorporated, and then add the orange zest and juice.

Pour the mixture into the prepared pan and bake for about 1 hour or so, until the loaf is risen and golden and a skewer inserted into the centre comes out clean. Leave to cool in the pan for 10 minutes, and then turn onto a wire rack to cool completely.

To make the topping, drizzle the melted chocolate over the top of the loaf and then scatter over the grated orange zest. Store in an airtight container.

Chunky Double Chocolate Bread

Makes 1 x 900 g/2 lb loaf
Preparation time 1¾ hours, plus cooling
You will need a loaf pan with a 900 g/2 lb/8-cup
capacity, lightly buttered and base-lined with baking
parchment or greaseproof paper

300 g/10 oz/2½ cups plain (all-purpose) flour
2 teaspoons baking powder
50 g/1¾ oz/⅓ cup (unsweetened) cocoa powder
300 g/10 oz/1¼ cups muscovado (dark brown) sugar
2 eggs, beaten
200 g/7 oz/1¾ sticks butter, melted and cooled
200 ml/7 fl oz/¾ cup milk
100 g/3½ oz/3½ squares dark (semi-sweet) chocolate,
    roughly chopped

This is a dark, deeply-flavoured chocolate loaf freckled with chunks of chocolate and made for spreading with cold, straight-from-the-fridge butter. A sort of second cousin to the muffin family, it makes a lovely treat at breakfast. It's also one of the loaves I often have in the freezer – frozen in slices packed between layers of baking parchment; they thaw beautifully at a moment's notice. Just pop a slice in the microwave on a low heat and serve warm with a dollop of whipped cream and a spoonful of strawberry jelly.

Preheat the oven to 180°C/350°F/Gas Mark 4. Sift the flour, baking powder and cocoa together into a large bowl. Stir in the sugar.

Mix the eggs with the butter and milk until thoroughly combined. Stir gently into the dry ingredients - take care not to over beat or the loaf will lose its nice texture. Fold in the chocolate chunks.

Spoon the mixture into the prepared pan and bake for about 1 hour 20 minutes, or until a skewer inserted into the centre comes out clean.

Remove from the oven and leave to cool in the pan for about 20 minutes. Turn onto a wire rack and leave until completely cold. Store in an airtight container.

Chocolate and Parsnip Loaf

Makes 1 x 900 g/2 lb loaf
Preparation time 1½ hours, plus cooling
You will need a loaf pan with a 900 g/2 lb/8-cup
capacity, lightly buttered and base-lined with baking
parchment or greaseproof paper

320 g/11 oz/2¾ cups plain (all-purpose) flour
1 teaspoon baking powder
1 teaspoon bicarbonate of soda (baking soda)
200 ml/7 fl oz/¾ cup sunflower (canola) oil
350 g/12 oz/1⅔ cups caster (superfine) sugar
100 g/3½ oz/⅓ cup black treacle (molasses)
3 eggs, beaten
100 g/3½ oz/½ cup dark (semi-sweet) chocolate chips
200 g/7 oz parsnip, grated

No curled up noses here please. Parsnips add oodles
of lovely flavour and texture to this loaf. Think carrot
cake and give it a try. You won't be disappointed.

Preheat the oven to 180°C/350°F/Gas mark 4. Sift the
flour, baking powder and bicarbonate of soda together into
a large bowl.

Beat the sunflower oil, caster (superfine) sugar, molasses
syrup and eggs together until smooth. Stir into the dry
ingredients and then beat in the chocolate chips and
grated parsnip.

Spoon the mixture into the prepared pan and bake for
about 1 hour 10 minutes, or until the loaf is nicely risen and
golden and a skewer inserted into the centre comes out clean.

Leave the loaf to cool in the pan for 20 minutes or so, and
then turn onto a wire rack and leave to cool completely.
Store in an airtight container.

Fresh Cranberry and Orange Loaf

Makes 1 x 900 g/2 lb loaf
Preparation time 1hour 10 minutes, plus cooling
You will need a loaf pan with a 900 g/2 lb/8-cup
capacity, lightly buttered and base-lined with baking
parchment or greaseproof paper

300 g/10 oz/2½ cups self-raising flour
2 teaspoons baking powder
175 g/6 oz/scant 1 cup caster (superfine) sugar
2 eggs,
200 ml/7 fl oz/1 cup milk
100 g/3½ oz/½ cup butter, melted and cooled
150 g/5 oz/¼ cup fresh cranberries
grated zest 1 orange
icing (confectioners') sugar, to dust

When it comes to cranberries in loafs, loaves and
cookies, I have to admit that I have a soft spot for
the chewy dried variety. Drying them intensifies the
taste and gives them a fabulous just-sweet-enough
taste. As a variation, this works beautifully with a
streusel topping, such as the one for Peach Streusel
Loaf on page 70.

Preheat the oven to 180°C/350°F/Gas mark 4. Sift the
flour and baking powder together into a large bowl. Stir in
the sugar.

In a separate bowl, whisk the eggs and milk together
with the cooled melted butter. Stir this mixture lightly
but thoroughly into the flour mixture and then fold in the
cranberries, taking care not to over mix.

Spoon the mixture into the prepared pan and bake for
about 50 minutes, or until golden and risen and a skewer
inserted into the centre comes out clean when removed.

Leave the loaf to cool in the pan for 15 minutes, and then
turn onto a wire cooling rack and leave until completely
cold. Store in an airtight container. Dust with icing
(confectioners') sugar to serve.

Cinnamon Swirl Quick Bread

Makes 1 x 900 g/2 lb loaf
Preparation time 1¼ hours, plus cooling
You will need 2 loaf pans, each with a 900 g/2 lb/8-cup
capacity, lightly buttered and base-lined with baking
parchment or greaseproof paper

350 g/12 oz/3 cups self-raising flour
2 teaspoons baking powder
85 g/3 oz/½ cup caster (superfine) sugar
5 tablespoons honey
300 ml/½ pint/1¼ cups milk
1½ teaspoons cinnamon

It's the swirl of cinnamon through this bread that
makes it special, so do remember to use a light
hand when folding the sweet honey syrup through
the batter.

Preheat the oven to 180°C/350°F/Gas mark 4. Sift the flour
and baking powder into a large bowl and stir in the sugar.
Gently heat 2 tablespoons of the honey with the milk and
pour into the flour, stirring until smooth.

In a separate small bowl, mix the remaining honey with
the cinnamon. Gently swirl the honey and cinnamon
mixture through the loaf batter to give a marbled effect.

Spoon the mixture into the prepared pan and bake for
about 1 hour, or until the loaf is golden and risen, and a
skewer inserted into the centre of the loaf comes out clean.

Leave to cool in the pan for 10 minutes or so, and then
turn onto a wire rack to cool completely. Store in an
airtight container.

Fragrant Orange and Cardamom Quick Bread

Makes two 450 g/1 lb loaves
Preparation time: 1 hour, plus cooling
You will need two 450 g /1 lb/4-cup loaf pans, each lightly buttered and base-lined with some baking parchment or greaseproof paper

8 green cardamom pods
2 large oranges
320 g/11 oz/2⅔ cups plain (all-purpose) flour
2 teaspoons baking powder
100 g/3½ oz/½ cup caster (superfine) sugar
2 eggs, beaten
200 ml/7 fl oz whole milk
100 g/3½ oz/⅓ cup butter, melted and cooled
icing (confectioners') sugar, for dusting

Preheat the oven to 180°C/350°F/Gas mark 4. Break open the cardamom pods and remove the tiny black seeds. Drop them into a mortar and crush lightly with a pestle. Set aside.

Grate the orange zest and reserve. Using a sharp knife, cut away the top and bottom of the oranges and then slice away the peel in a downward movement, taking care to remove all the bitter white pith from the orange flesh. Carefully cut away each segment, leaving behind the thin membrane in between. Cut each segment in half and set aside.

Sieve the flour and baking powder together in a large bowl, then stir in the sugar.

In a separate bowl, whisk the eggs and milk together with the butter. Stir them lightly but thoroughly into the flour mix and then stir in the orange zest and crushed cardamom seeds. Take care not to over-mix. Gently fold in the orange segments.

Divide the mixture between the prepared loaf pans. Bake for about 45 minutes, or until golden and risen. A skewer inserted into the centre should come out clean when removed.

Leave the cakes to cool in their pans for 15 minutes, and then turn out onto a wire cooling rack and leave until completely cold. Dust with icing (confectioners') sugar and serve immediately or store in an airtight container.

Toasted Raisin and Sultana (Golden Raisin) Bread

Makes 1 x 900 g/1 lb loaf
Preparation time 1¼ hours, plus cooling
You will need a loaf pan with a 2 lb/900 g/8-cup capacity, lightly buttered and base-lined with baking parchment or greaseproof paper

350 g/12 oz/3 cups self-raising flour
2 teaspoons baking powder
50 g/1¾ oz/⅓ cup golden caster (superfine) sugar
100 g/3½ oz mixed raisins and sultanas (golden raisins)
2 tablespoons golden (corn) syrup
300 ml/½ pint/1¼ cups milk

This loaf is a real favourite of mine toasted for breakfast or with a nice pot of tea following a long walk with the dog on chilly winter afternoons. The great thing about the recipe is that it just contains typical store cupboard ingredients that most of us will have easily to hand. Serve it freshly toasted with generous helpings of good butter.

Preheat the oven to 180°C/350°F/Gas mark 4. Sift the flour and baking powder into a large bowl. Stir in the sugar and the mixed fruit.

Gently heat the golden (corn) syrup and milk together (this will make it easier to mix) and then stir into the dry ingredients until thoroughly mixed.

Pour the mixture into the prepared pan and bake for about 50 minutes, or until the loaf is risen and golden and a skewer inserted into the centre comes out clean.

Leave to cool in the pan for 10 minutes or so, and then turn onto a wire rack to cool completely. Serve sliced and toasted with plenty of good butter. Store in an airtight container.

Pear and Chocolate Chip Loaf

Makes 1 x 900 g/2 lb loaf
Preparation time 1 hour 20 minutes, plus cooling
You will need a loaf pan with a 900 g/2 lb/8-cup capacity, lightly buttered and base-lined with baking parchment or greaseproof paper

300 g/10 oz/2½ cups self-raising flour
2 teaspoons baking powder
100 g/3½ oz /½ cup caster (superfine) sugar
2 eggs
200 ml/7 fl oz/1 cup milk
100 g/3½ oz/½ cup butter, melted and cooled
2 ripe but firm pears, cored and roughly chopped
50 g/1¾ oz/¼ cup dark (semi-sweet) chocolate chips

The combination of pears and chocolate is a classic; do use good-quality dark (semi-sweet) chocolate chips though. When baking with pears, it's important to choose fruit that is ripe but still firm. Pears that are over-ripe and very soft will ooze extra moisture into the mixture as it cooks and the result would be a heavy, sometimes even unpleasantly, soggy loaf.

Preheat the oven to 180°C/350°F/Gas mark 4. Sift the flour and baking powder together into a large bowl. Stir in the sugar.

In a separate bowl, whisk the eggs and milk with the cooled melted butter. Stir lightly but thoroughly into the flour mixture and then stir in the pears and chocolate chips. Take care not to over mix.

Spoon the mixture into the prepared pan and bake for about 1 hour, or until golden and risen and a skewer inserted into the centre comes out clean when removed.

Leave the loaf to cool in the pan for 15 minutes, and then turn onto a wire cooling rack and leave until completely cold. Store in an airtight container.

Spiced Easter Bread

Makes 1 x 900 g/2 lb loaf
Preparation time 1 hour 10 minutes, plus cooling
You will need a loaf pan with a 900 g/2 lb/8-cup
capacity, lightly buttered and base-lined with baking
parchment or greaseproof paper

350 g/11 oz/3 cups self-raising flour
2 teaspoons baking powder
1 teaspoon ground cinnamon
100 g/3½ oz/½ cup caster (superfine) sugar
150 g/5 oz/1 cup mixed dried fruit and chopped
    candied orange and lemon peel
2 tablespoons black treacle (molasses)
300 ml/½ pint/1¼ cups milk

The spices I've used in this loaf remind me of Easter.
It's another loaf that cries out to be toasted and
served hot with lots of cold butter, but there is no fat
in the batter. Fresh from the toaster, the bread takes
on a lovely moist and chewy texture.

Preheat the oven to 180°C/350°F/Gas mark 4. Sift the flour,
baking powder and cinnamon into a large bowl. Stir in the
sugar and the mixed fruit and peel.

   Gently heat the treacle (molasses) and milk together (this
will make it easier to mix) and stir into the dry ingredients
until thoroughly combined.

   Pour the mixture into the prepared pan and bake for about
50 minutes, or until the loaf is risen and golden and a skewer
inserted into the centre comes out clean. Leave to cool in the
pan for 10 minutes or so, and then turn onto a wire rack to
cool completely. Store in an airtight container.

New Orleans Pecan Bread

Makes 1 x 900 g/2 lb loaf
Preparation time 2½ hours, including cooking, cooling
and icing.
You will need a loaf pan with a 900 g/2 lb/8-cup
capacity, lightly buttered and base-lined with baking
parchment or greaseproof paper.

350 g/12 oz/3 cups self-raising flour
2 teaspoons baking powder
1 teaspoon ground cinnamon
100 g/3½ oz/½ cup light muscovado (dark brown) sugar
120 g/4 oz/1 cup pecans, roughly chopped
300 ml/½ pint/1¼ cups milk
2 tablespoons black treacle (molasses), slightly warmed

This is another recipe where a light toasting and a
little buttering highlights the delicious chewy texture
of the loaf. It also brings out the caramel flavours
created by the light muscovado (dark brown) sugar
and treacle (molasses).

Preheat the oven to 180°C/350°F/Gas mark 4. Sift the flour,
baking powder and cinnamon together into a large bowl. Stir
in the sugar, and then all but a small handful of the pecans.

   Beat the milk and warmed treacle (molasses) together
(warming the syrup will make it easier to mix) and stir into
the dry ingredients until thoroughly incorporated.

   Spoon the mixture into the prepared pan and scatter the
remaining pecans evenly over the top of the loaf. Bake for
about 1 hour, or until the loaf is risen and golden and a
skewer inserted into the centre comes out clean.

   Remove from the oven and leave to cool in the pan for
about 20 minutes. Turn onto a wire rack and leave until
completely cold. Store in an airtight container.

Orange and Rosemary Loaf

Makes 1 x 900 g/2 lb loaf
Preparation time 1¼ hours, plus cooling
You will need a loaf pan with a 900 g/2 lb/8-cup
capacity, lightly buttered and base-lined with baking
parchment or greaseproof paper

320 g/11 oz/2¾ cups plain (all-purpose) flour
2 tablespoons baking powder
150 g/5 oz/⅔ cup caster (superfine) sugar
200 g/7 fl oz/¾ cup milk
2 eggs, beaten
120 g/4 oz/1 stick butter, melted
grated zest 2 oranges
juice 1 orange
1 tbsp finely chopped fresh rosemary
icing (confectioners') sugar, for dusting

Rosemary is one of my favourite herbs and it works so
well in sweet recipes. This light orangey loaf is no
exception. I hope you like it as much as I do.

Preheat the oven to 180°C/350°F/Gas mark 4. Sift the
flour and baking powder together in a large bowl. Stir in
the sugar.

In a separate bowl, whisk the eggs and milk with the
cooled melted butter. Stir lightly but thoroughly into the
flour mixture and then stir in the orange zest and juice.
Take care not to over mix. Fold in the rosemary.

Spoon the mixture into the prepared pan. Bake for about
45 minutes or so, until golden and risen and a skewer
inserted into the centre comes out clean.

Leave the loaf to cool in the pan for 15 minutes, and then
turn onto a wire cooling rack and leave until completely
cold. Dust with icing (confectioners') sugar and serve
immediately or store in an airtight container.

Celebration Quick Breads

Iced Double Lemon Loaf

Makes 1 x 900 g/2 lb loaf
Preparation time 3 hours, including cooling and icing
You will need a loaf pan with a 900 g/2 lb/8-cup
capacity, lightly buttered and base-lined with baking
parchment or greaseproof paper

200 g/7 oz/¾ cup butter
300 g/10 oz/1½ cups caster (superfine) sugar
3 eggs, beaten
320 g/11 oz/2¾ cups plain (all-purpose) flour
200 ml/7 fl oz/¾ cup natural (plain) yoghurt
grated zest and juice ½ lemon

icing
grated zest and juice 1 lemon
350 g/12 oz/3 cups icing (confectioners') sugar

Calling all lemon fanatics... get your mixing bowl out
right now. This loaf is light, moist and utterly lip-
smacking. Why not double the recipe and make two
loaves to save any fighting over the last slice?

Preheat the oven to 180°C/350°F/Gas mark 4. Beat the
butter and sugar together until smooth and light. Beat in the
eggs, a little at a time, until fully incorporated (if the mixture
starts to curdle, add a little of the flour). Beat in the yoghurt
and lemon zest and juice.

Spoon the mixture into the prepared pan and bake for
about 1 hour 10 minutes, until golden and risen and a
skewer inserted into the centre of the loaf comes out clean.

Leave to cool in the pan for 10 minutes or so, and then
turn on a wire rack to cool completely.

To make the icing, sift the icing (confectioner's) sugar into
a bowl and stir in the lemon zest and enough juice to give a
thick but spreadable consistency. Pour over the loaf and
spread with a palette knife. Store in an airtight container.

Caribbean Coconut Bread

Makes 1 x 900 g/2 lb loaf
Preparation time 1½ hours, plus cooling
You will need a loaf pan with a 900 g/2 lb/8-cup
capacity, lightly buttered and base-lined with baking
parchment or greaseproof paper

320 g/11 oz/2¾ cups self-raising flour
200 g/7 oz/1 cup caster (superfine) sugar
2 teaspoons baking powder
½ nutmeg, grated
400 ml/14 fl oz/1⅔ cups coconut milk
2 very ripe bananas, mashed
1 egg, beaten

There's nothing particularly traditionally Caribbean about this loaf. It is just that the ingredients remind me of that part of the world and the fact that when I first made it I had just returned from a lovely working trip there, armed with nutmeg from the beautiful island of Grenada. The bread tastes lovely buttered and spread with honey.

Preheat the oven to 180°C/350°F/Gas mark 4. Mix the flour, sugar, baking powder and nutmeg together in a large bowl. In a separate bowl, whiz together the coconut milk, mashed bananas and egg. Stir into the dry ingredients until smooth.

Spoon the mixture into the prepared pan and bake for about 1¼ hours, or until risen and golden and a skewer comes out clean when inserted into the centre of the loaf.

Leave to cool in the pan for 10 minutes or so, and then turn out onto a wire rack and leave until completely cold. Store in an airtight container.

Very Berry Loaf

Makes 1 x 900 g/2 lb loaf
Preparation time 1½ hours, plus cooling
You will need a loaf pan with a 900 g/2 lb/8-cup
capacity, lightly buttered and base-lined with baking
parchment or greaseproof paper

250 g/9 oz/2¼ sticks butter
250 g/9 oz/1¼ cups caster (superfine) sugar
4 eggs, beaten
100 g/3½ oz/1 cup ground almonds
50 g/1¾ oz/½ cup plain (all-purpose) flour
100 g/3½ oz polenta
100 g/3½ oz/1 cup mixed raspberries and blueberries

Don't be concerned when the fruit sinks to the
bottom in this delicious loaf. Simply turn the loaf out
and serve the underneath uppermost, where all the
fruit will have formed a delicious irresistible layer.

Preheat the oven to 180°C/350°F/Gas mark 4. Cream the
butter and sugar together until light and fluffy. Add the
eggs, a little at a time, stirring well between each addition,
until the mixture is smooth and all the eggs have been
incorporated. Stir in the flour and polenta, and then fold
in the berries.

Spoon the mixture into the pan and bake for about 1¼
hours, or until golden and springy to the touch.

Remove from the oven and leave to cool in the pan for
about 20 minutes. Turn onto a wire rack and leave until
completely cold. Store in an airtight container.

Spiced Pumpkin Bread

Makes 1 x 900 g/2 lb loaf
Preparation time 1 hour 35 minutes, plus cooling
You will need a loaf pan with a 900 g/2 lb/8-cup capacity, lightly buttered and base-lined with baking parchment or greaseproof paper.

320 g/11 oz/2¾ cups plain (all-purpose) flour
1 teaspoon bicarbonate of soda (baking soda)
1 teaspoon ground ginger
200 g/7 oz/1 cup molasses sugar
100 ml/3½ oz/⅓ cup golden (corn) syrup
100 g/3½ oz/1 stick butter, melted
3 eggs, beaten
150 g/5 oz cooked pumpkin, puréed
100 g/3½ oz crystallized ginger, roughly chopped

This dense and spicy loaf works well using canned pumpkin, so don't just leave it until the pumpkin season to make.

Preheat the oven to 180°C/350°F/Gas mark 4. Sift the flour, bicarbonate of soda and ginger together into a large bowl and stir in the molasses sugar. Beat the golden (corn) syrup, butter and eggs with the pumpkin purée. Stir into the dry ingredients until thoroughly incorporated. Stir in the chopped ginger.

Spoon the mixture into the prepared pan and bake for about 1¼ hours, or until the loaf is risen and golden and a skewer inserted into the centre comes out clean.

Leave the loaf to cool in the pan for 15 minutes or so, and then turn onto a wire rack and leave until completely cold. Store in an airtight container.

Index

First published in 2005 by Conran Octopus Limited,
a part of Octopus Publishing Group,
2–4 Heron Quays, London E14 4JP
www.conran-octopus.co.uk

Publishing Director: Lorraine Dickey
Commissioning Editor: Katey Day
Editor: Sybella Marlow
Art Director: Jonathan Christie
Designer: Carl Hodson
Photography: Jean Cazals
Prop Stylist: Sue Rowlands
Home Economy: Liz Franklin
Production Manager: Angela Couchman

British Cataloguing-in-Publication Data.
A catalogue record for this book is available from
the British Library.

ISBN 1 84091 454 8

To order please ring Conran Octopus Direct
on 01903 828503

Printed and bound in China

Author's Acknowledgments
Sumo-sized thanks go out to the brilliant team at Conran
Octopus, in particular Katey Day and Sybella Marlow for
their editing expertise and for being such great people to
work with. To Jonathan Christie for creating a book that
looks every bit as edible as the recipes it contains, the lovely
Sue Rowlands for her brilliant styling, the handsome and
hugely talented Jean Cazals for his delicious photography;
and to all three for making the shoots so much fun. To my
loyal and lovely testers and tasters – my Mum and Dad and
the best bunch of friends anyone could wish for. And lastly,
to my three wonderful sons, Chris, Oli and Tim, whose
enthusiasm, support and willingness to eat never fades – with
oodles of love and a kiss for every crumb xx